THE
COMPLETE BOOK OF
Homemade Ice Cream,
Milk Sherbet, & Sherbet

THE
COMPLETE BOOK OF
Homemade Ice Cream,
Milk Sherbet, & Sherbet

CAROLYN ANDERSON

Illustrations by Deanne Hollinger

Saturday Review Press

New York

641.862
and

Published simultaneously in Canada by
Doubleday Canada Ltd., Toronto.

Library of Congress Catalog Card Number: 76–182479
ISBN 0–8415–0144–0

Saturday Review Press
230 Park Avenue, New York, New York 10017

Printed in the United States of America

Design by Tere LoPrete

To my husband
Gerald Lee Anderson

Contents

THE
COMPLETE BOOK OF
Homemade Ice Cream,
Milk Sherbet, & Sherbet

I

Introduction

"I Scream. You scream. We all scream for ice cream." At any age, in all seasons, the Good Humor bell, the ice cream coated dasher, or the announcement of ice cream for dessert elicits cries of delight. In America, ice cream is an almost certain part of everyone's childhood and current life. As a truck-stop treat and White House dessert, it is eaten and adored by people of all cultures and incomes.

Ice cream is, by far, America's favorite dessert. Americans can be proud of this, for it is due to our nation's productive dairy industry and rapid, continuous development of commercial ice cream manufacture that this rich, delicious, and nutritious dessert is available to all. Frozen confections that were once a luxury known only to kings and elite are today a standard American food and a delicious part of our prosperity.

Ice cream and cake is a lifelong birthday tradition. Americans have a sweet, and, I once read, a "cold" tooth, and perhaps there is something to the international fiction that the only time Americans are not eating ice cream is when they are chewing gum. No doubt ice cream is a part of many celebrations, happy moments, and daily occasions. It comes in more flavors than any other food, and the varieties of richness and smoothness, as well as modes of presentation, are seemingly endless. It is cooling in summer, refreshing and energizing in winter, and equally at home in a cone or crystal parfait glass. Though popularly a dessert, ice cream is eaten at any hour of the day. An "ice cream for breakfast" movement gained followers in the 1940s, and a national cereal company may be currently renewing this movement. They have produced a breakfast product containing freeze-dried ice cream and cereal tasting like cones.

The current news in ice cream though is the rapidly growing desire of Americans for old-fashioned homemade ice cream. A year ago the sale of ice cream freezers was reported to be increasing, and the movement continues to grow. Local housewares stores now carry the newest electric and hand-turning models and old, old-fashioned models are beginning to appear in antique shops. Old-fashioned ice cream has come back in fashion. Today, not in lieu of, but in addition to the abundant good commercial ice cream, Americans yearn for homemade ice cream. Making ice cream makes a party!

Many people have treasured and abundant memories of old-fashioned ice cream. Though in the past three decades homemade ice cream may have been reserved for special events, the art has not been lost. For many people, the very mention of homemade ice cream brings forth a lovely taste evoking descriptive history: Grandfather, let me turn the dasher. . . . Those hot summer Sunday afternoons . . . the four-gallon freezer at the church social . . . ripe strawberries from the garden and morning's milk . . . Many sympathize with the statement from *Mrs. Appleyard's Kitchen*: "Think of the arid childhood of one who has never been handed the dash, . . . a bowl, and a spoon, and

who actually, in the melting sweetness, never finds a shred
of peach or strawberry. . . . Let's not think of it—too sad."

Ice cream reminiscences are especially delightful because
they can be closely reexperienced today. We may open the
ice cream freezer on a modern city terrace rather than
under the old oak tree, but the joy in making the ice cream
and the taste of it is just the same as it was in our
great-grandfather's day. And, for our children, these
current days of ice cream making will be their memories.

II

History of Ice Cream and Sherbet

Ice cream making is an ancient art with a history intertwined with great men and world events. However, as is true in the origin of many arts, frozen ice and cream was most likely a development of many men spread across the far corners of the world, and spanning centuries of time. The references through history are fascinating, though incomplete in evidence and evolutional ties.

Legends exist from the fourth century B.C. that Alexander the Great had a special fondness for iced beverages. Then, centuries later, iced delicacies were apparently coveted by the Roman emperors. Great feasts included chilled wines, and fruit juices frozen with ice and snow. This was an incredible feat, for the snow and ice were carried from the Alps to Rome. Relays of slave runners raced through the heat with their heavy load in order that it might reach the tables of the rulers. For the Caesars, plans to have iced desserts needed to be made at least a month before the meal, and strategy for transport was a general's dilemma. Nero, known for his fierce cruelties in his reign from A.D. 54 to 68, was no less monstrous in the record of ice cream history. When the runners did not make it to Rome before the snow melted, he is said to have executed the general in command.

Meanwhile, in the Orient, fragrant ices were being devoured with equal fervor. These ices, forerunners of modern sherbets, consisted of fruit juices or liqueurs mixed with crushed ice. Such cooling delicacies were served at ancient Chinese, Indian, Persian, and Arabian banquets. Whether the idea spread from dynasty to dynasty or rose simultaneously is unknown. At any rate, the East gave full approval to sherbet and made continued refinements in flavors and textures. Sherbets became appetizers and digestives, and it was felt that they were almost a necessity as an interim course for soothing and revitalizing the stomachs of the gourmands.

In his famous travels from 1271 to 1295, Marco Polo observed the sherbet habit. He returned to tell Europe of the cushion-seated men devouring frozen concoctions following feasts of meat. All this was not idle talk, for Marco had brought back recipes for frozen marvels, and the sherbet habit soon spread throughout Italy. Possibly some of these imported recipes may have included milk and were similar to contemporary milk sherbets. Though lineage is lost, milk, cream, and other products began to be used and ice beverages, water ices, and sherbets were soon joined with what was called "cream ice" or "butter ice"—close relatives in the family tree of ice cream.

Catherine de Medici of Florence is credited with giving Frenchmen the lovely Italian gift of ice making. When she married Henry II of France in 1533, she took her pastry cooks and ice cream makers with her to Paris. News spread to the French populace of the delicious delicacy, but for more than a hundred years recipes were carefully guarded and tasting was a privilege of a select few within the Louvre or Royal Palace. Sharing his mother's love for this regal treat, Henry III was such an avid enthusiast that he apparently ate ices every day.

Louis XIV's chef, Vatel, who was known for his creation of exotic dishes, was so clever in his preparation of frozen creams that there are occasional references to Vatel as the inventor. Although not the inventor, Vatel surely did not disappoint the great Louis XIV when, as a guest described, he served ice cream at banquets in the following manner: "Toward the end of the feast, his chef caused to be placed before each guest, in silver gilt cups, what was apparently a freshly laid egg, colored like those of Easter, but before the company had time to recover from their surprise at such a novelty at dessert, they discovered that the supposed eggs were delicious sweetmeats, cold and compact as marble." Under Vatel, creamy frozen desserts reached a pinnacle of splendid, regal perfection.

English contemporaries were certainly keeping pace with the French. Although some records indicate frozen sweets moved through royal channels from France to England, a very informed Englishman might retort that iced delights were known to them in 1191, placing them considerably ahead of the French. Richard the Lion-Hearted is reported to have eaten sherbet while on a Holy Crusade in the East. Whether he returned from his romantic ventures with recipes seems now unknown. However, in later centuries, English royal history has definite reference to frozen cream ices. During the reign of King Charles I, his famed chef prepared a frozen concoction similar to modern ice cream. This dish pleased the king so much that, in approximately 1640, the king declared the recipe should be kept forever a royal secret. To accomplish this end, King Charles paid off the cook with a pension of 500 pounds a year. But history marches on, and King Charles' life and the secret were both of short duration.

At the end of the seventeenth century, commoners in France and England were thoroughly ready for a share in this taste treat, and for their satisfaction small ice cream shops began to open. Café Procope opened in Paris on Rue de l'Ancienne Comédie in 1660. This shop, one of the first, was run by an Italian from Palermo. Italians continued their influential role in ice cream development, and, in 1798, a well-known Italian, Tortoni, took over an ice cream shop in Paris at Number 10 on the Boulevard des Italiens. His Biscuit Tortoni and a host of other delicious and elegantly molded desserts gained fame throughout Europe. The popular ice cream salons of the eighteenth century were scenes of fashionable rendezvous and delicious sweets.

Sherbets and ice creams were a part of America's rich heritage from Italy, France, and England. In the same way that settlers left their old worlds to become Americans, this imported frozen sweet gradually took on citizenship to such a degree that it has become our national dessert.

Though our country's democratization of ice cream is complete today, the beginning of ice cream in our country was similar to that of the royal courts of Europe. Only the most elite colonists could afford the extravagance of buying ice for freezing cream. The first patent on a refrigerator was not issued until 1803; therefore, during many early decades of America's development, ice cream maintained its elevated luxurious status, symbolic of wealth and prosperity. Tasting iced cream desserts was a new, unusual experience for many colonists. William Black, guest of Governor Bladen of Maryland, described a dinner of 1744: "We had a dessert no less curious; among the rarities of which it was compos'd was some fine ice cream which, with the strawberries and milk, eat most deliciously." This description seems oddly reminiscent of Marco Polo's first encounters with the exotic frozen concoctions of the East. Perhaps due to his enthusiasm, Mr. Bladen is often credited with the origin of the phrase "ice cream."

Our early Presidents enjoyed sherbets and ice creams. George Washington was known to have two pewter ice cream pots, and ice cream eating at Mount Vernon was a very pleasant part of his private life. No doubt pleasing to our first President was a dinner served to him by the wife of the first secretary of the treasury, Mrs. Alexander

Hamilton. Mrs. Johnson, a guest at her dinner, described "pyramids of red and white ice cream with punch and liquors, rose, cinnamon and parfait amour." For some ice cream historians, Mrs. Hamilton was the leader in popularizing ice cream in the United States.

Radically disagreeing with the choice of Mrs. Hamilton are the fans of Dolley Madison. To them the lovely, pink-cheeked, charming wife of our fourth President was the true American patroness of ice cream. Tantalizing are the images of this famous hostess and her frozen creations. Strawberry ice cream was the crowning glory of her husband's second inaugural ball in 1812. A guest, in admiration, wrote, "Mrs. Madison always entertains with grace and charm, but last night there was a sparkle in her eye that set astir an air of expectancy among her guests. When finally the brilliant assemblage—America's best—entered the dining room, they beheld a table set with French china and English silver, laden with good things to eat, and in the center, high on a silver platter, a large shining dome of pink ice cream." No wonder hostesses throughout America wished to imitate Dolley.

The White House was not the only stage for spectacular feasts and frozen concoctions. In 1794, when General Wayne defeated the Indians at the Battle of Fallen Timbers in northwestern Ohio, he reported that he and his officers, "waiting only long enough to wash away travel stains, sat at a table to dine sumptuously on roast venison, beef, boiled mutton, duck, raccoon, o'possum, mince and apple pies, plum cake, floating island, and to cap the jubilation, dishes of ice cream. . . ." Ice cream was spreading through the land in the eighteenth century, and shops for frozen confections were beginning to bring the treat to the populace.

In America, Philip Lenzi, in 1774, was the first to announce publicly that he had set up a shop where ice cream was available in New York. He advertised in the New York *Gazette* that he had the necessary preparations to supply the gentry with confections, including ice cream.

Ice cream required a special order, but perhaps demand was increasing, for in 1777, Lenzi again advertised that he had moved his shop to Hanover Square and he then said, "May be had almost everyday, ice cream."

Competition grew. Mr. J. Crowe provided ice cream at No. 120 Hanover Square in New York. Mr. Joseph Crowe advertised in 1786 that "ladies and gentlemen may be supplied with ice cream every day at the City Tavern by their humble servant, Joseph Crowe." The Louisiana *Courier* carried an advertisement in 1808 stating that "ice cream may be had at the Coffee House every day between the hours of 12 and 9 o'clock." These small, scattered shops with hand-churned ice cream were the first glimmerings of the booming retail business of today.

The sweeping advance of ice cream from a rarity to common food began in 1851, when Jacob Fussell, a milk dealer, began to manufacture ice cream in Baltimore. It has been said that Mr. Fussell started a little snowball rolling down a long hill and it is still getting bigger. Following his tremendously successful Baltimore venture, Fussell opened a plant in Washington, D.C., in 1856, a plant in Boston in 1862, and a plant in New York in 1864. In 1858, a student of Fussell's, Perry Brazelton, opened a plant in St. Louis.

As plants opened and spread to all cities, mechanical advancements were occurring too, at a rapid rate. Hand manufacturing gave way to mass production, due to better equipment and techniques. Inventions such as the homogenizer (1899), the circulating brine freezer (1902), the direct expansion freezer and continuous freezing process (1913), dry ice for transportation (1925), the Vogt continuous freezer (1928), home storage freezers (1940), plus accurate testing equipment, conveyors, packaging machinery, and refrigerated trucks were tremendously significant in the industry's development.

Today, modern, immaculate plants are filled with vast amounts of efficient machinery. The ice cream mix is continually pumped into one end of the machine and, under pressure, in a matter of seconds it is whipped, frozen, injected with fruits, nuts, or whatever, automatically packaged, sent to hardening rooms, into refrigerated trucks, and on to consumers. Ice cream manufactured almost instantaneously in huge amounts would seem miraculous to any man who remembers the early ice cream factories. One of Iowa's early manufacturers remembered that on the Fourth of July in 1890, his plant delivered 300 gallons of hand-churned ice cream to celebrating Americans. What a job this must have been! Now the United States is the undisputed international leader in current ice cream production. The demand of the American public for ice cream is limitless and insatiable.

"Store boughten" ice cream and sherbet comes in a myriad of shapes, sizes, and brands. The historical development of today's abundant variety is closely matched with the industry's improved techniques for mass production and portability. Except for some small push carts, such as the hokey-pokey salesmen used before the commercial industry developed, ice cream was usually sold "straight" in confectionery shops.

The ice cream soda and ice cream sundae came into being at the end of the 1800s. Several claim the fame of inventing these treats, and it is likely that more than one person simultaneously created them. Fred Sanders of Detroit, Michigan, is often mentioned as the inventor of the ice cream soda. It is said that in 1879 he discovered his cream was sour, and to meet his hot clients' demands for the usual soda mixture of carbonated water, fruit juice, and sweet cream, he substituted ice cream, and the public was overjoyed.

Evidently, the ice cream sundae developed as an evasion tactic. Strict local blue laws forbade serving ice cream sodas on Sunday. One of the clever drugstore operators who was reported to have devised the sundae was a man in Evanston, Illinois. On the Sabbath, he served noncarbonated syrups on the ice cream and called it a "Sunday soda." Fearing that it might be sacrilegious to use the name of a holy day across the counter, "sundae" soon

evolved. Sundaes soon challenged and won in popularity with the soda. The somewhat Puritan beginnings of the sundae, with its touch of syrups on a scoop of ice cream, is amusing in light of its later development. In the last two decades, famous sundaes such as "Lover's Delight," a huge affair served in a pineapple shell with four ice cream flavors, a variety of syrups, mounds of whipped cream, nuts, cherries, and a real gardenia to top it off, as well as equally stupendous creations known as "Trophy," "Flaming Maiden," "Ting-a-ling," "Virgin's Delight," "Hopalong Cassidy," "Screwball's Delight," and "Suicide Special," have periodically graced menus across the country.

Portable sidewalk treats were also glamorized and popularized in the early 1900s. Ice cream cones were invented at a St. Louis fair in 1904. Apparently, Mr. E.

Hamwi, a Syrian waffle salesman, noted that a neighbor vendor at the fair had run out of dishes for selling his ice cream. Clever Mr. Hamwi rolled his thin waffles into cone shapes, which hardened as they cooled. These eatable holders, filled with ice cream, so pleased the crowds that they immediately became an established practice and widespread treat. Other portable elaborations, such as the Eskimo Pie invented by C. Nelson of Iowa in 1921, the Good Humor sucker patented by the Harry Burt family of Ohio in 1923, and the Popsicle created by Epperson of California in 1926, and many variants of these inventions, are now so generally accepted that imagining they once did not exist is difficult.

The Good Humor sucker was so named because of a then popular theory that the humor of the mind was regulated by the humors of the palate. The early wrappings illustrated a sobbing, empty-handed child on one side and a happily ice cream-eating child on the other side. If this belief were fact, the American temperament would be continually content.

Soft ice cream sold from trucks, and from conveniently located roadside stores, was created by Tom Carvel. He perfected and patented in 1939 an electric freezer to produce a product that is soft rather than firm, and with a slightly higher temperature than ice cream. Also, his machine would produce soft ice cream in the quantity needed at the time of sale. Carvel became a millionaire, and his and other similar soft ice cream chains cover the United States.

With the vast number of types and brands of ice cream, a need for some state regulating laws developed. In one metropolitan area alone, a consumer report study in 1959 found more than 130 brands on the market. Although these products vary considerably in fat content, food solids, and weight per gallon, the consumer is protected by certain minimum legal standards. These minimum standards are important in ice cream manufacture since ice cream can be simulated rather closely by cheaper and nutritionally inferior ingredients. In addition, standards limiting the amount of overrun ensure that the purchaser will get a high-quality product. Overrun is the amount of air whipped into the ice cream. The maximum desirable overrun in ice cream is 100 percent, which means the ice cream mix is doubled in volume with air. The consumer might be unable to detect a higher percentage of air in a smooth-textured but inferior product; consequently, a weight minimum is set for products labeled "ice cream." A weight minimum of 4.5 pounds per gallon and a total food solids minimum of 1.6 pounds per gallon might be an expected weight of commercial ice cream with 100 percent overrun. Minimum butterfat content is generally somewhere in the range of 8 to 14 percent.

Products not meeting legal ice cream standards may be sold in some states under other names. "Ice milk" is an example of a product in which the butterfat content of most brands is under 6 percent but labeled clearly. The public does not confuse it with ice cream, and it is often a choice of consumers interested in a low-calorie product. Mellorine products, which represent the "margarine" of the ice cream world, are sold in a few states. Mellorine was developed in approximately 1955. It is similar to ice cream except that vegetable or non-dairy animal fat is substituted for milk fat.

In the United States, not only is ice cream currently a popular dessert, but also it is of significant economic importance. The ice cream industry uses approximately 7.6 percent of all the milk produced in this country. When milk production is at its highest during the summer months, the surplus is used by the ice cream industry, and for this reason the ice cream industry is often called the balance wheel of the dairy industry.

The ancient art of sherbet and ice cream making has survived through the centuries. Though exact origins are uncertain and ties in its evolution are lost, enough references through history remain to prove its worldwide spread and function as a pleasure-giving delicacy. As technology has improved in the modern age, the ice-cream-making art has advanced to a highly developed state. Inevitably, progress will continue in order to meet the public's demands for ice cream and sherbet.

III

How to Make Homemade Ice Cream, Milk Sherbet, and Sherbet

Ice Cream Makers

Early ice cream makers, such as those used by George Washington's or Dolley Madison's servants, were called "pot freezers." The container of sweetened cream was agitated by hand in a pan of salt and ice until the cream was frozen. In 1846, an American housewife, Nancy Johnson, invented the hand-crank freezer, which is still in use in similar form today. By turning a handle, the ice cream mix is churned within a container that is submerged in a bucket of ice and salt. An article in *Good House-keeping* magazine in July, 1911, described the best freezers as those having wooden pails, usually made of pine staves held in place by welded hoops and with well-made metal cylinders. Wood was used because it is a non-conductor of heat and also because the ice and salt would not corrode the wood. Metal for the inside containers was desirable because it was a conductor of heat. This construction was based on the principle that the heat from the cream would pass through the metal to the ice and salt, but the wood would protect the ice from melting from the heat of the room. A hand-crank freezer of this construction works well. Its modern counterpart works on the same principles, except that new materials, such as heavy plastic, have replaced wooden buckets.

Ice cream makers available today for churn-frozen ice cream are generally one of three types:

1. *Hand-Crank Tub Freezer*

This freezer consists of a large tub and center cylinder. The crank is attached to the agitator dasher and the cylinder. The dasher rotates in one direction and the cylinder rotates in the opposite direction. Cranking of the dasher is done by hand. The tub is packed with ice and salt.

2. *Electric Tub Freezer*

This freezer consists of a large tub and a center cylinder containing a dasher. An electric motor revolves the can around the dasher. The tub is packed with ice and salt.

3. *Refrigerator-Tub Ice Cream Freezer*

This freezer is a small unit consisting of an electric motor attached to scrapers in a container for the ice cream mix. The unit is placed in the freezer of the refrigerator, and the freezer door is closed on a flat electric cord. Ice and salt are unnecessary.

Ice cream makers vary in size. The 1- or 2-gallon freezer is typically the model displayed in stores, but freezers may range from 2 cups to 4 or 6 gallons. Though called ice cream makers, the same machines are used for making sherbets and milk sherbets.

Still-frozen ice cream is made without a special freezer. The ice cream mix is poured into a freezer tray, loaf pan, or mold and placed in the freezing compartment of a refrigerator.

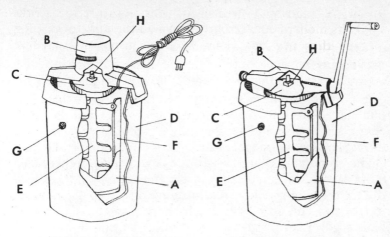

ELECTRIC-POWERED FREEZER
a) freezer can
b) motor
c) freezer-can cover
d) freezer tub
e) dasher
f) dasher paddle
g) drainage hole
h) freezer-can cover hole

HAND-CRANK FREEZER
a) freezer can
b) hand-crank gear
c) freezer-can cover
d) freezer tub
e) dasher
f) dasher paddle
g) drainage hole
h) freezer-can cover hole

Ice and Salt

Ice and rock salt are essential in making ice cream or sherbet in a hand-crank tub freezer or an electric tub freezer. More questions are raised about the function of ice and salt than about any other area of ice cream making. A typical question is: "Salt is used on sidewalks to make ice melt in winter; how can it make ice cream freeze?" Also, many questions are raised about whether the proportion of ice to salt makes a difference in freezing.

Definitely, salt melts ice. It is this process which is utilized in ice cream making. Ice alone, which has a temperature below 32° F, absorbs a specific amount of heat when it melts. To melt the ice faster and thus increase the amount of heat that it absorbs in a given time, salt is added. By adding 25 percent of salt by weight, temperatures may be obtained as low as $-10°$ F. The ice and salt packed around the container rapidly absorb the heat of the ice cream mix, so that freezing of the mix occurs.

Rock salt, sometimes called ice cream salt, is the same salt that is often used for sprinkling on icy sidewalks. It is coarse salt and should be used in ice cream freezing instead of regular fine white table salt.

The proportion of ice to salt does make a difference. The more salt that is added, the faster the ice melts, the faster the ice cream mix is lowered in temperature, and the faster it freezes. The speed with which the ice cream mix is frozen governs to a great extent the resulting texture and volume of the ice cream. Although quicker results are obtained by a large proportion of salt, a finer quality of ice cream is produced by a moderate proportion, causing slower freezing, which allows the mix to be sufficiently churned.

The amount of churning also influences the texture. As the mixture begins to freeze, it forms little crystals of ice throughout. The turning dasher whips and breaks up these finely divided particles into a smooth-frozen mixture that is preferable to a coarse, rough-textured consistency, which would result without sufficient agitation. In addition, the longer the dasher must turn before the mixture freezes, the more air is incorporated. Air is important in ice cream, just as air is necessary in a loaf of bread or a soufflé. Aeration or "overrun" in homemade churn-whipped ice cream should be somewhere around 25 percent. The air increases the frozen volume and it adds to its smooth, light quality. Ice cream without air whipped into it at some point in its preparation would be a sullen, heavy mass. However, the whipping, freezing process must not be slowed down to the point that freezing does not occur before the ice cream mix is whipped into butter. For this reason, the recommended proportion of salt to ice is a "moderate" one. Freezing should be neither too slow nor too fast.

In practical terms, "moderate" salt-ice ratio translates to approximately four parts ice to one part rock salt. This proportion is, of course, measured by volume, not by weight.

With the ratio of 4 to 1, freezing of the mix takes somewhere in the vicinity of 20 minutes. Variation in the length of freezing time may be due to the consistency and sweetness of the mixture, the temperature of the mixture when it is placed in the freezer can, the churning speed, and the outside surrounding temperature. Slight variation in freezing time due to these factors is not reason for alarm. However, before freezing, some consideration of the sugar content of the ice cream mix is advisable, since sugar retards freezing. If a very sweet mixture is used, a greater proportion of salt to ice to speed freezing would be desirable.

The hand crank and the electric tub freezers are packed in an identical way. The ice must be in small enough pieces so that it will not jam the freezer in the turning process. Block ice is easily crushed by placing it in a burlap bag and beating it with a hammer or mallet. Small ice cubes or purchased crushed ice may also be used. The freezer should first be filled one-third full of ice. Then salt and ice should be added in alternating layers until the freezer is full. If the salt is too close to the bottom of the tub, it will quickly melt the bottom layer and then not have as much action on the remaining ice. The salt is therefore more completely utilized if it is placed in layers in the upper two-thirds of the tub. A similar proportion of ice and salt should be used in packing the outside tub for ripening the ice cream. Ripening means letting the ice cream remain in freezing conditions for at least 1 hour so that flavors blend and the ice cream hardens.

How to Churn-Freeze

Churn-Freeze: The ice cream or sherbet mix is continuously stirred by mechanical apparatus while freezing.

Instructions:

1. Prepare ice cream or sherbet mixture according to recipe instructions. Refrigerate the mix until ready to freeze.

2. Crush the ice into fine pieces.

3. Measure rock salt in amount needed for a ratio of 1 part salt to 4 parts ice.

4. Put the dasher in the freezer can, and fill the can ⅔ full of ice cream or sherbet mixture.

5. Fit the can into proper position in the tub.

6. Pack freezer tub with crushed ice and rock salt. Tub should first be filled ⅓ full of ice, then salt and ice added in alternating layers until freezer is full.

7. Begin rotation of the mix. In an electric maker, motor should be started, allowing can to revolve for 2 minutes before packing tub. Rotate mix in hand-crank freezer slowly at beginning of freezing process and as rapidly as possible when cranking begins to be laborious. When crank cannot be turned without great difficulty, stop churning. Disconnect motor of electric maker when the motor begins to "labor."

8. Open can, allowing it to remain in tub. Remove dasher. Press ice cream or sherbet down in the can. Cover top of can with a layer of tinfoil. Replace can lid. Plug hole in can top. (Carefully avoid getting any surrounding ice and salt into the can.)

9. Ripen the ice cream or sherbet for 1 hour or more. To ripen, pour water from freezer and repack with additional ice and salt, covering the top of freezer can. Wrap tub in burlap or newspapers. (Alternate method of ripening: Remove can from tub. Place in freezing compartment of refrigerator for 1 hour.)

10. Serve.

How to Still-Freeze

Still-Freeze: The ice cream or sherbet mix is frozen without churning. No special ice cream maker is required.

Instructions:

1. Prepare ice cream or sherbet mixture according to recipe instructions.
2. Pour mix into desired refrigerator ice tray or mold, and freeze without stirring in freezing compartment of refrigerator.*
3. Serve.

Some still-frozen mixes are removed from the freezer, beaten by hand, and returned to the freezer, but this is specified in the recipe directions. Generally, the texture of still-frozen ice creams is good only if sufficient air has been whipped into the mix prior to freezing, or at some point during the freezing. In most cases, churn-freezing, if possible, will create a better product.

IV

Classification and Ingredients of Frozen Desserts

As the recipes in this book illustrate, a vast variety of ingredients can be used in making ice cream and sherbet. Likewise, there are myriads of classifications for these frozen desserts. Often, however, these categories are overlapping and meaningless. Comparison shows that names for frozen desserts such as frappes, granitas, ices, mousses, parfaits, or even names of the various ice creams themselves—Philadelphia, French, American—do not indicate any clearly distinguishable differences. These terms are often used inconsistently and their vagueness leaves many recipes fitting into several categories. According to some definitions, parfaits are light ice creams of a less cold and more creamy nature; frappes are partly frozen sherbets; mousses are parfaits frozen to the center; granitas are water ices with a gritty texture; and American ice cream is a less rich custard with fewer egg yolks than French ice cream. Classifications of such a refined nature seem best only for esoteric or cosmetic functions. There are only three basic categories: ice cream, milk sherbet, and sherbet. In my classification, sherbet is distinguished from ice cream because it contains no milk or cream. The category of milk sherbets is not so clearly distinguished, and they might best be included in the ice cream section since they contain milk. However, the separation is maintained since they are basically sherbets in which milk has been substituted for a proportion of the water. There is some difference in taste and texture between milk sherbets and both sherbets and regular ice cream.

The following ingredients are frequently used in ice cream, milk sherbet, or sherbet:

Cream is the part of the milk that floats to the top of the milk while it is standing, or is removed from the milk by means of a centrifugal separator. It contains a heavy concentration of butterfat. According to Federal Food and Drug standards, heavy whipping cream should have a minimum of 36 percent fat, and light, coffee, or table cream should have 18 percent to 30 percent fat. Cream is the best source of butterfat in ice cream and the more fat, the richer and smoother the ice cream will be. Cream also has the quality of making the mix whip readily, as well as giving a good flavor. Half and half, which is a mixture of milk and cream, can generally be substituted for light cream, but depending on local standards, it may have a slightly lower milk fat content. It may vary from approximately 10 percent to 12 percent. As cream is whipped, air is forced into the cream, causing the film of milk protein that holds the fat globules together to coagulate and to form a continuous stable, foamy structure. In homemade churn-type ice cream making, heavy cream should generally be only lightly whipped prior to freezing, since too great coagulation might result in a buttery texture.

Milk is a source of butterfat as well as milk solids for ice cream and milk sherbet. The butterfat content of milk enhances the richness and flavor of the ice cream, and the milk proteins bind the ice cream together, preventing a coarse texture. When milk is required in homemade ice cream and milk sherbet receipes, homogenized milk should be used. In homogenized milk, the fat globules and nonfat milk solids are broken up into smaller particles and blended. This process aids the production of a smoother dessert.

Sweetened condensed milk is a concentrated canned milk that is preserved with sugar. Evaporated milk is also a concentrated milk that has about 60 percent of the water removed from it. Evaporated milk does not have sugar added, but instead it is preserved by a heat treatment after it is canned. In ice cream and milk sherbet, evaporated milk may be substituted for fresh milk without other recipe changes. Use of condensed milk, however, may require a reduction in the amount of sugar in the mix. Since concentrated milks have so much water removed, they may be used in mixes where there are other ingredients with high water content, thus decreasing the possibility of ice granules forming from the water when freezing. Concentrated milks, used in abundance, may give a caramelized flavor to the frozen dessert.

Since the milk product used often forms a greater proportion of the mix, its taste will often alter the flavor of the resulting product, since milk does not always have the same taste. Milk can be flavored by the foods eaten by the cow and it is also susceptible to absorption of strong odors within the household refrigerator. Thus, before using, the milk product should be taste-tested for sweetness and freshness.

Sugar, usually granulated cane or beet sugar, gives the necessary quality of sweetness to the ice cream, sherbet, or milk sherbet. Sugar also functions to lower the freezing point of the mix. This allows more churning to occur before freezing, causing more air to be incorporated and thus giving a smoother-textured product. Sweetness in ice cream is to be desired, and a mix generally should not have less than 12 percent sugar. On the other hand, too much sugar may keep the mix from getting firm and it may diminish one's sense of refreshment. In some blends, sugar may reduce the intensity of certain flavors such as chocolate.

Sweetening effects can be varied by the use of brown sugar, maple sugar, corn syrup, honey, or saccharin. Brown sugar consists of fine sugar crystals coated with molasses. Maple sugar is maple sap that is cooked until it turns to syrup and finally into crystallized sugar. Corn syrup is made from cornstarch, and it sweetens as well as aids in the production of a firm, creamy product. Honey is, of course, a natural sweetener, and ice cream flavors can be varied in interesting ways by the type of honey used. Saccharin is manufactured from toluene, derived from coal tar, and it, as well as other sugar substitutes, can be used in place of sugar in the proportion recommended in the package instructions.

Salt of the ordinary table type is used in very small quantities in ice creams. The salt brings out the flavor and the sweetness of the frozen mix. In ice creams that are made with eggs or nuts, salt rather noticeably serves to enhance the flavor. In most ice creams, though, the amount of salt added should be so small that the presence or absence of it would be difficult to detect in tasting. A salty ice cream is a disaster.

Eggs are often used in ice creams, sherbets, or milk sherbets. The egg yolk has the ability to form stable emulsions. Besides flavor, egg yolks in the mix may create a faster whipping mix, a firmer, better texture, and a richer ice cream. When eggs are used, generally the yolks are separated from the whites. In custard bases, the yolks are combined and cooked with the milk or cream. If the whites are whipped and folded into the mix prior to freezing, aeration and smoothness of the product is enhanced.

Stabilizers are optional ingredients in ice creams, sherbets, and milk sherbets. The main function of a stabilizer is to help keep the texture of ice cream from changing during storage. Stabilizers either work to combine with water as water of hydration or form gel structures in water, thus slowing down the growth of ice crystals, which occur in some mixes if they are not eaten immediately. Stabilizers also aid in the creation of a smooth-textured ice cream that has a resistance to melting. Milk and cream are natural stabilizing materials and for this reason commercial stabilizers are not always necessary. Gelatin, fruit pectins, and milk casein products are commercial stabilizers often used in homemade ice cream. Gelatin is a product made from animal bones, skins, and connective tissues, and it is interesting to note that these are the same materials used in making glue!

V

Ice Cream Dieting and Nutritive Value

For anyone worried about his diet, this should be a conscience-soothing section. Ice cream is a highly nutritious food that can be used to gain weight or to lose weight. To gain weight, ice cream should be added to a regular diet. To lose weight, ice cream should be eaten as a basic part of a regular diet. The idea of gaining weight is easily visualized, since ice cream is often served in a supplementary way in the form of pie à la mode, ice cream cones, and fudge sundaes; and in such combinations with already high-caloric foods it is a natural boost to weight increase. The idea of ice cream for slenderizing may seem less obvious.* It is essential in this plan that ungarnished ice cream be substituted for other food in the normal diet. The ice cream with its proteins, minerals, and vitamins is good for the body, and, ungarnished, it is often lower in

---

* Marion White wrote a book on Ice Cream Diets in 1946. He describes how ice cream can be eaten two to three times a day with weight loss.

calories than many commonly eaten foods. The number of calories in a serving fluctuates considerably, due to the composition of the mix. However, an average serving of ice cream (1/12 of a quart) has about 100 calories. Naturally for a reducing diet, ice cream, low in sweetness and butterfat, or milk sherbet or sherbet are the best frozen dessert choices.

The food value of ice cream as an integral or supplementary part of the diet is best illustrated in a summation of the nutrient content of ice cream. Ice cream is an excellent source of calcium and phosphorus, much needed minerals for growth of strong bones and teeth, and of milk proteins, the easiest of the food proteins to digest. It also contains vitamin A, vitamin B_1, or thiamine, and vitamin B_2, or riboflavin, as well as other vitamins. Vitamin A is especially important in the body for increasing night vision and is good for the skin. The fact that ice cream is a good source of riboflavin is appropriate and desirable, since riboflavin gives energy and is known as a "youth-promoting" vitamin.

Despite all the health aspects of ice cream, most people want to eat ice cream for the sheer pleasure of it. For this reason, mothers who wish to increase their children's milk intake find ice cream a pleasant solution. Ice cream is frequently served in hospitals, and doctors have discovered that even very hard to please patients will eat it without complaining. In fact, patients are probably often unaware that the ice cream may be a part of a carefully prescribed diet to aid recovery.

VI

Helpful Hints

In the making and eating of lots of ice cream, milk sherbet, and sherbet, I have discovered a number of small but often very interesting bits of information and helpful tricks. I offer these miscellaneous hints here.

1. A fork is the best tool for digging into ice cream that is too firm to scoop. A cake breaker is good for slicing firm ice cream.

2. If no cooking is required, often the ingredients can be combined right in the freezer can, which means fewer dishes to wash.

3. If ice cream is to be hand-stirred during freezing, or if it is to be removed from one container to another, use a wooden spoon to prevent transfer of heat from the hand to the mix.

4. Always allow space in the freezer can for expansion of the ice cream when it freezes. Approximately 1/3 of the can is needed for the swell.

5. Cool the mix to room temperature or slightly lower before freezing. Churn-freezing a warm mix may cause a buttery texture due to an increased freezing period.

6. Cardboard milk cartons are good containers for making block ice.

7. Rock salt can be saved for later use by pouring the used ice and salt mixture into a burlap sack. Let the ice melt to leave the salt.

8. Ice cream is at its best in the first week it is made and it cannot be stored for more than 1 month without losing its original texture and flavor. Wrapping containers of ice cream in aluminum foil aids in prolonged storage.

9. Ice cream should be stored at 0° F, but to enhance the flavor of firmly frozen cream it should be placed in the lower section of the refrigerator for approximately 15 minutes before serving. Ice cream should be 12° F when served.

10. Freezing decreases the strength of most flavorings, so flavorings should be used plentifully in frozen desserts.

11. Extracts, fruits, and liqueurs lose some of their flavor if added to a warm mixture. They should usually be added when the mixture has cooled.

12. Lemon juice enhances fruit flavors in frozen desserts and keeps many fruits from darkening, but it should be used sparingly.

13. Puréed fruit increases distribution of the fruit through the mix and decreases the possibility of ice crystals forming around larger fruit pieces.

14. Canned fruits are often sweeter than fresh fruits and some adjustment in the sugar content of the mix may be needed. Also, canned fruits should usually be drained before using.

15. Custards tend to curdle if cooked too long and if the temperature is too hot or uneven. Stirring constantly and using a double boiler are important in custard making. If curdling occurs, remove from the heat and beat the custard vigorously.

16. Lightly whipping ingredients such as egg whites or cream before adding them to the mix makes a creamier frozen product.

17. If chocolate is used in a mix, heating the chocolate with any other liquid creates a better blend than is possible by adding chocolate to a previously heated liquid. Lumps in heated chocolate and milk can be removed by beating with a rotary beater. To enhance a chocolate flavor, omit vanilla.

18. To eliminate last-minute serving details, ice cream can be scooped ahead of time, and the balls stored in the freezer.

19. Chill serving dishes for 5 minutes in the freezer if the frozen dessert is not too firm.

20. To marbelize a parfait, alternate layers of ice cream and sauce, and then run a knife up and down the inside of the parfait glass.

21. To decorate ice cream, work on a cookie sheet over a pan of ice.

22. One quart of ice cream is needed to fill a 9-inch pie shell. The pie shell should be completely cooled before ice cream is added.

23. If liqueur is used as an ice cream topping, usually only a small amount, approximately ½ ounce per serving, is needed.

Special Note

Some of the recipes in this book are marked with a check mark before the title. The check mark is to draw your attention to recipes I have found to be especially delicious.

VII

How to Mold Ice Cream and Sherbet

Molded frozen desserts are glamorous. Inevitably, guests are impressed when shaped ice cream is served, and it seems that few people are informed about the actual simplicity of molding. I have tried packing ice cream into most every kind of metal container in my kitchen. Coffee cans, kettles, pudding pans, and salad molds make excellent ice cream molds. Bombe molds and individual serving molds made especially for ice cream molding are also available. In addition, I have discovered that cake molds in the shape of animals, Santa Claus, and houses work beautifully for ice cream, too. My favorite cake mold for ice cream consists of two intricately detailed doves perched on a mound. The doves in blueberry on a mound of vanilla surrounded by spun sugar on a silver tray make a marvelous sight. This creation is far more exciting than scoops of ice cream, yet it requires very little additional preparation time.

To mold a frozen dessert, follow the following procedures:

1. Put the empty mold in the refrigerator freezer while the ice cream or sherbet is being prepared.

2. As soon as the frozen mix is ready to be ripened, quickly transfer it from the freezer can to the cooled mold. (If previously frozen ice cream is being used, let it soften slightly. Sherbet need not be softened since it is naturally pliable.)

3. With a spoon, press the ice cream or sherbet into the mold, being certain no large air spaces remain inside.

4. If more than one flavor is to be used in the same mold and sharp dividing lines are desired, freeze each layer until it is firm before adding another flavor. To keep ice cream on the side of a mold but not in the middle, as is desired in a bombe, the ice cream may be pressed upwards as it begins to harden. I have also found it convenient to press a deep bowl upside down in the center of the bombe, thus forcing the ice cream upwards on the sides. The bowl is removed when the second layer is added.

5. Cover the mold with foil and freeze the molded ice cream or sherbet overnight, or until it is very firm.

6. To unmold, quickly immerse the mold in a pan of lukewarm water, or let cool faucet water briefly run over it. Cover the top of the mold with a cooled serving tray and then turn it all upside down so that the ice cream will be released on the tray. If the sherbet or ice cream is not released immediately, shake it slightly, and if necessary wipe the mold with a hot, wet dish towel. Inserting a knife at one point along the edge of the mold allows some air to enter and aids in releasing the frozen form.

VIII

Fancy Ice Cream Desserts and Accompaniments

For many men and women, culinary work is a creative, rewarding experience. Homemade ice creams, milk sherbets, and sherbets, though delicious ungarnished, can be turned into splendiferous creations in the hands of the imaginative. Molding, decorating, and combining ice cream with other sweets can be done in an endless number of ways.

A popular frozen spectacular is the bombe. Contrasting colors and flavors of ice cream or sherbet are combined in definite layers in a fancy molded "bombe" shape. Bombes were originally made to resemble round bombs once used in battles. Realism was carried out by serving the unmolded iced ball with a flaming brandy-soaked wick on the top. Sherbet is often used for the outside layer of the bombe, while the inside is often a rich mixture such as a custard-based ice cream.* Raspberry sherbet with vanilla ice cream, chocolate with pink peppermint or butter pecan, strawberry with orange, and pistachio with coconut are a few of the huge variety of bombe combinations.

* See section VII, How to Mold Ice Cream and Sherbet.

Akin to the bombe is the Baked Alaska. This creation consists of a mound of ice cream on a layer of yellow sponge cake, or any favorite plain cake, with an overall coating of meringue, lightly browned from baking. Any flavor ice cream can be used in a Baked Alaska, but strawberry is often chosen, probably because of its lovely color. The ice cream should be packed into a mold with a top diameter equal in size to the layer of cake. Freeze the ice cream in the mold until very firm. Preheat the oven to 500° F. Soak in cold water a wooden board large enough to hold the cake. Remove the board from the water and cover it with heavy paper. Place the cooled layer of cake on top of the paper-covered board. Prepare a meringue by beating 6 egg whites until stiff and then folding ¾ cup confectioners' sugar into the whites. Unmold the ice cream onto the layer of cake, and quickly cover the ice cream and cake with meringue. Swirl the meringue into peaks. Place the board and all into the oven and bake for approximately 5 minutes, or until all the peaks have turned light brown. The board, paper, and cake do not conduct the heat, and the ice cream will not melt. Though simple to make, this frozen-baked combination is innately fascinating.

Cakes can take on new heights when combined with ice cream. A two-layer cake can be glamorized into a seven-layer spectacular by splitting each layer and adding layers of ice cream between cake. Visualize a white cake with layers of lemon ice cream topped with orange frosting, or chocolate cake with alternating layers of peppermint and vanilla ice cream covered with thick chocolate icing. Layered ice cream cakes can be made ahead of time, wrapped, and frozen. Approximately 15 minutes prior to serving they should be placed in the lower part of the refrigerator to soften slightly. For smaller cake treats, cupcakes can also be split, filled with ice cream, wrapped, returned to the freezer, and kept ready for snacks or last-minute guests.

A lovely ice cream and sherbet mock cake can be made in an angel food cake pan. Make round scoops of several different ice creams and sherbets such as pistachio, cherry, and orange. Place the scoops separately in the freezer and freeze until they are very firm. When firm, arrange the scoops, alternating flavors, in the angel food cake pan. Over each circle of scoops pour a vanilla ice cream mixture prepared by softening vanilla ice cream, adding lots of nuts and chocolate chips, and beating in an electric mixer. The vanilla mixture ties the scoops together. After freezing until firm, it can be unmolded and topped with whipped cream and even birthday candles.

Ice cream cake rolls can be made with a variety of ice cream and cake flavors. The cake should be of a jelly roll-type sponge cake, and it should be baked in a paper-lined jelly roll pan measuring about 15 by 10 by 1 inch. Immediately after baking the cake, turn it upside down on a hot, damp cloth, remove the paper, and then roll up the cake and towel together. When the cake is cool, unroll, remove towel, spread cake with slightly softened ice cream, reroll, and then freeze until firm. My favorite ice cream cake roll is made with chocolate cake and vanilla ice cream. To make the cake, sift together ¼ cup of flour, 1 cup confectioners' sugar, 3 tablespoons cocoa, and ½ teaspoon salt. Separate 10 eggs. Beat egg yolks until thick and then, while beating, gradually add the sifted mixture. Beat the egg whites until stiff and then fold beaten egg whites and 1 teaspoon vanilla extract into the egg yolk mixture. Bake for approximately 20 minutes in a 400° F oven.

Ice cream and sherbet make good pie fillings, too. Graham cracker or pastry crusts, filled with a favorite ice cream, are especially attractive when topped with sliced fruits, meringue, or whipped cream. To add variety, nuts or sauces can be swirled into the ice cream before filling the pie shell. Mincemeat blended with softened vanilla, refrozen in the pie shell, topped with meringue, and then baked for a few minutes is a splendid example of an old-fashioned pie modernized.

Ice cream profiteroles are another rich pastry dessert. These creations are simply small cream puffs filled with ice cream and topped with any ice cream sauce. To make cream puffs, combine ½ cup butter with 1 cup water in a saucepan. Heat to boil. While beating vigorously, gradually add 1 cup flour to the hot mixture. Continue to stir on medium heat for about 1 minute while the mixture sticks together. Remove from heat and beat 4 whole eggs into the dough. Beat until well blended. Drop by teaspoonfuls, 3 inches apart, onto a cookie sheet. Bake at 450° F for the first 10 minutes and at 350° F for the remaining 20 to 30 minutes. The puffs should be dry and toasty brown in color. After they have cooled, cut off the tops, remove any insides, and fill with ice cream.

Parfait, meaning "perfect," is a term sometimes used to classify certain ice cream mixtures that are still-frozen. However, more popularly, *parfait* refers to a dessert served in tall "parfait" glasses and made of tiny scoops of ice cream or sherbet with ingredients such as sauces, liqueurs, fruits, nuts, or whipped cream surrounding the scoops. Parfaits are best prepared and stored in the freezer an hour or more before serving, which makes them ideal for a glamorous ready-to-serve dessert.

Sundaes are usually not prepared in advance of serving, but like parfaits, they are made of scoops of ice cream with one or many kinds of dressings such as sauces, fruits, nuts, and whipped cream. The following sauces are a few of the many good ones for parfaits and sundaes.

Fudge Sauce

In top of double boiler, over hot water, combine 3½ ounces of semisweet chocolate with 3 tablespoons butter. On medium heat, cook, stirring, until well melted. Add ⅓ cup dark corn syrup. Stirring occasionally, let mixture simmer for 15 minutes. Stir in 1 teaspoon vanilla extract and ½ teaspoon instant coffee. Serve hot or cold.

Chocolate Peanut Butter Sauce

In a saucepan, mix together 1 cup canned chocolate syrup with ½ cup crunchy peanut butter. Cook, stirring, until blended. Serve warm or cool.

✓ Chocolate Marshmallow Sauce

In a saucepan, combine 1¼ cups brown sugar, ½ cup milk, and ½ cup cocoa. On medium heat, cook, stirring, until sugar melts and mixture is well blended. Remove from heat and stir in 1 tablespoon butter, ½ teaspoon vanilla, and 1 cup small-sized marshmallows. Serve warm or cool.

Mocha Sauce

In a saucepan, combine 2½ teaspoons instant coffee, 1 cup evaporated milk, and 1 cup canned chocolate syrup. Cook, stirring, until mixture comes to a boil. Cool.

Coffee Sauce

In a saucepan, combine 1 cup strong coffee liquid with 1 tablespoon flour. On medium heat, cook, stirring, until mixture thickens. Cool. Beat in ½ cup heavy cream and 1 teaspoon vanilla extract.

✓ Blueberry Sauce

In a saucepan, combine 2 teaspoons cornstarch, ¼ cup sugar, 1½ teaspoons fresh lemon juice, ⅛ teaspoon nutmeg, and ¼ cup water. Cook, stirring, until mixture comes to a boil; then, stirring occasionally, let mixture simmer for 5 minutes. Add 1 package thawed frozen blueberries (10-ounce size), undrained. Cook, stirring, until well combined. Serve warm or cold.

Orange Sauce

Mix together, without cooking, ¾ cup honey, ¼ cup fresh orange juice, and 2 teaspoons finely grated orange rind.

✓ Strawberry Sauce

In a saucepan, combine 1 cup strawberries, 3½ tablespoons sugar, and 1½ tablespoons fresh lemon juice. Cook, stirring, until well blended. Shake together 2 teaspoons cornstarch with 2 tablespoons water, and add to mixture in a saucepan. Let mixture boil for 2 minutes. Cool.

Cherries Jubilee Sauce

In a chafing dish, heat to a boil juice from 1 can Bing cherries (30-ounce size). Shake together 5 teaspoons cornstarch, ¼ cup cold water, and 5 teaspoons granulated sugar, and add to juice in chafing dish. Mix well. Add cherries. Continue to heat, stirring, for 5 minutes. Add ½ cup warmed brandy and flame. Serve immediately.

Butterscotch Sauce

In a saucepan, mix together ¾ cup brown sugar, ⅓ cup light corn syrup, and 2 tablespoons butter. Cook, stirring, until well blended. Cool. Beat in ½ cup heavy cream.

Maple Syrup Sauce

In a saucepan, combine 1½ cups maple syrup with ½ cup heavy cream. Cook, stirring, until well blended. Cool.

Melba Sauce

In a saucepan, combine 1 cup fresh raspberries, ¾ cup red currant jelly, and ¾ cup sugar. Stirring occasionally, let mixture simmer for 5 minutes. Strain. Shake together 1½ tablespoons cornstarch with 3½ tablespoons water and add to raspberry-currant mixture. Cook, stirring, until thickened. Cool.

Grape Sauce

In a saucepan, combine 1¼ cups canned grape juice with ⅓ cup light corn syrup. Cook, stirring, until mixture comes to a boil; then, stirring occasionally, let mixture simmer for 10 minutes. Then add 1 tablespoon butter. Cool. (Optional: add ¼ teaspoon cinnamon.)

Peppermint Sauce

In a saucepan, combine ½ cup crushed peppermint candy, ¾ cup water, and ½ cup light corn syrup. On medium heat, cook, stirring, until candy melts. Shake together 1 tablespoon cornstarch with 2 tablespoons water and add to the peppermint mixture. Cook, stirring, until thickened. Cool.

Wine Sauce

Combine, mixing well, ⅓ cup red wine or claret with ½ cup light corn syrup.

Rum Sauce

Combine 1 cup confectioners' sugar with one beaten egg yolk. While beating, add 4 to 5 tablespoons rum. Fold ¾ cup whipped heavy cream and 1 teaspoon vanilla extract into the mixture.

IX

Ice Cream

√ **World-Famous Philadelphia Vanilla**

6 cups light cream   ⅛ teaspoon salt
1¼ cups granulated sugar
2 vanilla beans (3-inch
    size), split

1. In top of double boiler, combine 3 cups cream, the sugar, vanilla beans, and salt. Cook, stirring constantly, for 10 minutes. Remove beanpods, scraping pulp and seeds into the cream. Cool.
2. Add remaining 3 cups cream to the cooled mixture. Mix well.
3. Churn-freeze.

Makes ½ gallon

A key recipe—use your imagination and add fruits, nuts, and flavorings to make this vanilla into your own concoction.

World's Richest Ice Cream:
Truffled Ice Cream

2 truffles	⅛ teaspoon salt
4 egg yolks, beaten	6 cups heavy cream
¾ cup granulated sugar	

1. Wash truffles in warm water. Cut truffles into very small squares.
2. In top of double boiler, combine truffles, beaten egg yolks, sugar, salt, and 1 cup of the heavy cream. Beat with rotary beater until blended. Then cook, stirring constantly, until mixture thickens slightly. Cool.
3. Add remaining 5 cups cream.
4. Churn-freeze.

Makes ½ gallon

Truffled ice cream can be made with either the black truffle of France or the white of Italy. A black-truffle ice cream called "Black Diamond" was once prepared by Lorenzo Delmonico of Delmonico Restaurant for three famous gourmets, August Belmont, Leonard Jerome, and William Travers. In the early 1900s this ice cream was served at the most lavish and fashionable dinners. Today, the Scalini Restaurant in Rome serves a white-truffle ice cream.

World's Most Exotic Ice Cream:
Flower Ice Cream

4½ cups light cream
1½ cups granulated sugar
 6   egg yolks, beaten
 ¼   teaspoon orange
      flower water

¼ cup dried jasmine
    petals
¼ cup fresh jonquil
    petals
¼ cup fresh pink
    (dianthus) petals

1. In top of double boiler, combine 1 cup of the light cream, the sugar, and beaten egg yolks. Beat with rotary beater until blended. Then cook, stirring constantly, until mixture thickens. Remove from heat.

2. Add orange flower water and petals of jasmine, jonquils, and pinks. Stir. Let stand for 15 minutes. Strain and cool.

3. Add remaining 3½ cups light cream to the strained flower mixture.

4. Churn-freeze.

Makes ½ gallon

These rather special ingredients can be fairly easily obtained at specialty stores. In the New York area, orange flower water can be bought at Trinacria Importing Company, 415 Third Avenue, New York, N.Y. 10016, and dried jasmine at Kiehl Pharmacy, 109 Third Avenue, New York, N.Y. 10003. Fresh jonquils and pinks can be bought at the florist if you do not grow them in your own garden.

Almond Ice Cream

1 cup granulated sugar
⅛ teaspoon salt
8 egg yolks, slightly
  beaten
3 cups light cream
1½ cups heavy cream,
  lightly whipped

1 pound blanched
  almonds, finely
  chopped
½ teaspoon almond
  extract

1. Stir together sugar, salt, and slightly beaten egg yolks.
2. In top of double boiler, add light cream to sugar mixture and cook, stirring constantly, until mixture coats a spoon. Cool.

3. Add lightly whipped heavy cream, finely chopped almonds, and almond extract to cooled custard.

4. Churn-freeze.

Makes ½ gallon

Almond Crisp Ice Cream

2 tablespoons salad oil
½ cup brown sugar, firmly packed
½ cup salted peanuts, chopped
2 cups crisp rice cereal
½ cup honey

1 teaspoon almond extract
1 teaspoon vanilla extract
4 eggs, beaten
3 cups evaporated milk

1. In top of double boiler, combine salad oil, brown sugar, peanuts, and cereal. Cook, stirring occasionally, until sugar melts. Remove this crumb mixture from heat.

2. Add honey, almond extract, and vanilla extract to the beaten eggs and beat with rotary beater until well mixed.

3. Add evaporated milk to egg mixture. Mix well.

4. Stir crumb mixture into egg-milk mixture.

5. Churn-freeze.

Makes ½ gallon

Applesauce Ice Cream

3 cups sweetened applesauce
1 cup granulated sugar

¼ cup fresh lemon juice
3½ cups heavy cream, whipped

1. Combine applesauce, sugar, lemon juice, and whipped heavy cream. Mix well.

2. Still-freeze to a mush.
3. Beat.
4. Still-freeze until firm.

Makes ½ gallon

Apricot Ice Cream I

4 *cups canned apricots,*   1½ *cups granulated sugar*
   drained and mashed   2 *cups heavy cream*

1. Combine mashed apricots and the sugar. Let stand for 3 hours in the refrigerator.
2. Lightly whip cream and fold into apricots.
3. Churn-freeze.

Makes ½ gallon

Apricot Ice Cream II

2 *pounds fresh apricots*   1 *cup evaporated milk*
2 *cups water*   1 *teaspoon grated lemon*
1 *cup granulated sugar*   *rind*
2 *cups heavy cream,*   ½ *teaspoon almond*
   whipped   *extract*

1. In a saucepan, combine apricots and water. Cook, on low heat, for 10 minutes.
2. Add sugar to apricots and continue to cook for 10 more minutes.
3. Press apricot mixture through a sieve to remove skins and stones. Cool.
4. Add whipped heavy cream, evaporated milk, lemon rind, and almond extract to the apricot purée.
5. Churn-freeze.

Makes ½ gallon

Apricot Ice Cream III

1½ cups granulated sugar
 1 cup water
 6 egg whites
 ¼ teaspoon salt

3 cups heavy cream,
   lightly whipped
2½ cups canned apricots,
   drained and chopped

1. In a saucepan, combine sugar and water. Boil for 5 minutes.
2. Beat egg whites with salt until stiff.
3. Gradually pour hot sugar water over egg whites and beat until cool.
4. Add lightly whipped heavy cream and chopped drained apricots to egg white mixture.
5. Churn-freeze.

Makes ½ gallon

Apricot Almond Ice Cream

1½ cups dried apricots
 1 cup water
 2 cups milk
 2 eggs, slightly beaten
 1 cup granulated sugar
 ⅛ teaspoon salt

1 teaspoon vanilla
   extract
½ teaspoon almond
   extract
2 cups heavy cream,
   lightly whipped

1. In a saucepan, cook dried apricots in water.
2. In another saucepan, mix together milk, slightly beaten whole eggs, sugar, and salt. Cook, stirring, until mixture coats a spoon. Cool.
3. Add vanilla extract, almond extract, apricot pulp with juice, and lightly whipped cream to the cooled milk mixture.
4. Churn-freeze.

Makes ½ gallon

Apricot Orange Ice Cream

1 cup canned apricots, with syrup	⅛ teaspoon salt
1½ cups fresh orange juice	1 cup granulated sugar
1 tablespoon fresh lemon juice	4 cups heavy cream, lightly whipped

1. Drain apricots, reserving syrup. Add orange juice, lemon juice, salt, and sugar to syrup.
2. Purée apricots (press through sieve or use electric blender).
3. Combine syrup mixture, apricots, and lightly whipped cream.
4. Churn-freeze.

Makes ½ gallon

Avocado Ice Cream

2 teaspoons unflavored gelatin	1¼ cups granulated sugar
2 tablespoons water	⅛ teaspoon salt
4 ripe avocados, peeled	4 cups heavy cream, lightly whipped
¼ cup plus 2 tablespoons fresh lemon juice	

1. In top of double boiler, soften gelatin in water for 5 minutes. Then heat until dissolved.
2. Purée avocado pulp in an electric blender, adding lemon juice, sugar, and salt to the avocado while puréing.
3. Combine dissolved gelatin, avocado mixture, and lightly whipped cream. Mix well.
4. Still-freeze (or churn-freeze).

Makes ½ gallon

Baked Apple Ice Cream

3 cups baked apple pulp, puréed (about 12 medium-size apples)	1½ tablespoons fresh lemon juice
3½ cups heavy cream	¼ teaspoon ground nutmeg
1 cup granulated sugar	¼ teaspoon ground cinnamon

1. Peel and core apples. Bake in covered baking dish in 350° F oven for 45 minutes. Purée in electric blender on medium speed.

2. Combine cream, baked apple purée, sugar, lemon juice, nutmeg, and cinnamon.

3. Churn-freeze.

Makes ½ gallon

Banana Ice Cream I

1 cup granulated sugar	5 large bananas
¼ teaspoon salt	1½ tablespoons fresh lemon juice
5 egg yolks, slightly beaten	2 cups heavy cream
3 cups light cream	

1. In top of a double boiler, stir together sugar, salt, slightly beaten egg yolks, and 2 cups of the light cream. Cook, stirring frequently, until mixture coats a spoon. Cool.

2. Peel and mash bananas and combine with lemon juice.

3. Add heavy cream, remaining light cream, and bananas to the cooled egg yolk mixture.

4. Churn-freeze.

Makes ½ gallon

Banana Ice Cream II

3 Junket rennet tablets	6 bananas
3 tablespoons cold water	2 tablespoons fresh lemon juice
4 cups light cream	1½ cups heavy cream, lightly whipped
1½ cups granulated sugar	

1. Dissolve rennet tablets in cold water.
2. Heat light cream and sugar until lukewarm (110° F).
3. Add dissolved rennet tablets to light cream mixture and let stand at room temperature for 10 minutes.
4. Peel and mash bananas and combine with lemon juice.
5. Add bananas and lightly whipped heavy cream to rennet mixture.
6. Churn-freeze.

Makes ½ gallon

Try banana ice cream in a banana split. Due to its high sugar and vitamin content, the banana is one of our most important fruits.

√ Banana Marshmallow Ice Cream

1 cup milk	1 teaspoon fresh lemon juice
30 marshmallows	
¾ cup granulated sugar	3½ cups heavy cream
3 cups sliced bananas (about 4 bananas)	

1. In an electric blender, combine milk, marshmallows, sugar, sliced bananas, and lemon juice. Blend on high speed.

2. Whip heavy cream and then stir cream into blended banana mixture.

3. Still-freeze.

Makes ½ gallon

Banana Orange Ice Cream

7   very ripe large bananas
4   teaspoons fresh lemon
    juice
¼   teaspoon salt
1   cup granulated sugar

1½ cups fresh orange juice
¼   cup confectioners'
    sugar
3   cups heavy cream,
    lightly whipped

1. Peel and mash bananas and combine with lemon juice, salt, granulated sugar, and orange juice.

2. Fold confectioners' sugar into lightly whipped heavy cream and add to banana mixture.

3. Churn-freeze.

Makes ½ gallon

Barefoot Vanilla

2   tablespoons flour
¾   cup granulated sugar
2   eggs, beaten
2   cups light cream
1   teaspoon vanilla
    extract

¼   teaspoon lemon
    extract
½   cup condensed milk
4   cups heavy cream

1. Sift together flour and sugar and then combine with eggs.

2. In a saucepan, heat light cream to a boil.

3. While stirring vigorously, add the egg mixture to the hot light cream. Cook, stirring, on medium heat until slightly thickened. Cool.

4. Add vanilla extract, lemon extract, condensed milk, and heavy cream to the cooled mixture.

5. Churn-freeze.

Makes ½ gallon

Going barefoot was strictly forbidden until May First on my grandmother's Indiana farm. But as soon as the calendar turned, our shoes came off and there were many hot barefoot days when my brother and I, with our cousins, eagerly watched Grandmother come out of the house with a crock of this cream and pour it into the freezer that Granddad cranked. This is a wonderful American custard ice cream!

Biscuit Tortoni

4 cups heavy cream, whipped	2 cups crumbled macaroons
1 cup confectioners' sugar	2½ tablespoons dry or sweet sherry
4 egg whites, stiffly beaten	

1. Combine whipped heavy cream, confectioners' sugar, stiffly beaten egg whites, finely crumbled macaroons, and sherry. Mix well.

2. Still-freeze.

Makes ½ gallon

Blackberry Ice Cream

1¾ cups granulated sugar	1 teaspoon fresh lemon juice
1 cup water	
3 cups fresh blackberries	3 cups heavy cream

1. In a saucepan, combine sugar and water. Boil 5 minutes. Cool.

2. Purée blackberries in an electric blender.

3. Combine sugar syrup, blackberry purée, and lemon juice. Let mixture stand for 1 hour. Strain to remove berry seeds.

4. Add heavy cream to strained blackberry mixture.

5. Churn-freeze.

Makes ½ gallon

Black Cherry and Rum Ice Cream

1 cup milk	1½ cups heavy cream
3 egg yolks	3 cups chopped fresh
½ cup granulated sugar	black cherries
¼ teaspoon salt	2 tablespoons rum

1. In top of double boiler, heat milk to a boil.

2. Beat together egg yolks, sugar, and salt and add slowly, while stirring vigorously, to the hot milk. Cook, stirring, until thickened. Cool.

3. Add heavy cream, chopped cherries, and rum to the cooled mixture.

4. Churn-freeze.

Makes ½ gallon

Black Walnut Ice Cream

1½ cups granulated sugar	2 teaspoons vanilla
¾ cup water	extract
¼ teaspoon salt	3 cups heavy cream,
3 egg whites, stiffly beaten	whipped
2 cups black walnuts, finely chopped	

1. In a saucepan, combine sugar, water, and salt. Boil for 5 minutes.

2. In bowl of electric mixer, beat egg whites on medium speed until peaks form. Then beat on high speed while slowly pouring hot sugar syrup into egg whites. After syrup is added, continue to beat on low speed for three minutes.

3. Fold chopped walnuts, vanilla, and whipped cream into the egg white mixture.

4. Churn-freeze.

Makes ½ gallon

√ Blueberry Ice Cream

2 pints fresh blueberries
1 cup granulated sugar
⅛ teaspoon salt

2 cups heavy cream, lightly whipped
1 cup evaporated milk

1. Mash berries and cook with sugar, on medium heat, stirring constantly, for 5 minutes.

2. Press berries through a sieve. Cool.

3. Add salt, lightly whipped heavy cream, and evaporated milk to the berries.

4. Churn-freeze.

Makes ½ gallon

√ Brandy Honey Ice Cream

1½ cups honey
6 cups evaporated milk

¼ teaspoon salt
½ cup brandy

1. Heat honey until lukewarm.

2. Combine evaporated milk and honey. Beat with rotary beater until blended.

3. Add salt and brandy to honey mixture. Cool.
4. Churn-freeze.

Makes ½ gallon

Brown Bread Ice Cream

¾ cup granulated sugar
⅛ teaspoon salt
4 egg yolks, slightly
  beaten
2 cups light cream

1½ cups dried Boston
  brown bread crumbs
3 cups heavy cream
1 teaspoon vanilla
  extract

1. Stir together, until well mixed, sugar, salt, and slightly beaten egg yolks.
2. Add light cream to egg yolk mixture and cook, stirring constantly, in top of double boiler until mixture coats a spoon. Cool.
3. Soak brown bread crumbs in heavy cream for 15 minutes.
4. Add vanilla and bread crumb mixture to egg yolk mixture.
5. Churn-freeze.

Makes ½ gallon

Burnt Almond Ice Cream

3 cups evaporated milk
1¼ cups granulated sugar
1 tablespoon cornstarch
1 tablespoon cold milk
¼ teaspoon salt
2 teaspoons vanilla
  extract

2 cups heavy cream,
  lightly whipped
1½ cups chopped
  blanched, toasted
  almonds

1. In top of a double boiler, heat evaporated milk.
2. Caramelize the sugar. (To caramelize sugar, put sugar in a heavy skillet and cook, stirring constantly over medium heat—338° F—until sugar turns to a golden brown syrup.)
3. Combine, mixing well, cornstarch and cold milk.
4. Add caramelized sugar, salt, and cornstarch mixture to the hot milk in top of the double boiler. Cook, stirring, until thickened. Cool.
5. Add vanilla, lightly whipped cream, and almonds. (To toast almonds, place in a frying pan and cook, stirring continuously, on medium heat for 5 minutes.)
6. Churn-freeze.

Makes ½ gallon

Burnt Walnut Ice Cream

1⅓ cups granulated sugar
1½ cups chopped walnuts
3 egg yolks, slightly beaten
⅛ teaspoon salt
2 cups light cream
¾ tablespoon vanilla extract
2 cups heavy cream, lightly whipped

1. Caramelize 1 cup of the sugar. (To caramelize sugar, put sugar in a heavy skillet and cook, stirring constantly over medium heat—338° F—until sugar turns to a golden brown syrup.)
2. Add chopped walnuts to the hot caramelized sugar. Allow walnut sugar mixture to cool in a lightly buttered pan. When cool, pound, using mortar and pestle, until finely ground.
3. In top of double boiler, combine, mixing well, egg yolks, remaining ⅓ cup sugar, and the salt.
4. Heat to a boil the light cream and, while stirring, add the hot cream slowly to the egg yolk mixture in top of double boiler. Cook until mixture thickens. Strain through a sieve and cool.

5. Add vanilla extract, ground nut mixture, and lightly whipped heavy cream to the cooled custard.

6. Churn-freeze.

Makes ½ gallon

Burnt Sugar Ice Cream

1¾ cups granulated sugar   1½ cups milk
 5   cups heavy cream

1. Caramelize sugar. (To caramelize sugar, put sugar in a heavy skillet and cook, stirring constantly over medium heat—338° F—until sugar turns to a golden brown syrup.)

2. Add 2 cups of the heavy cream to caramelized sugar and continue cooking, stirring constantly, until blended. Cool.

3. Add remaining cream and the milk.

4. Churn-freeze.

Makes ½ gallon

√ Butter Pecan Ice Cream I

 1   cup finely chopped   ¾   cup granulated sugar
     pecans   2   tablespoons vanilla
 2   tablespoons butter   extract
2½ cups heavy cream   2   cups milk

1. In a skillet, brown the pecans in the butter. Cool.

2. Mix together the browned pecans, cream, sugar, vanilla, and milk.

3. Churn-freeze.

Makes ½ gallon

Butter Pecan Ice Cream II

1½ cups finely chopped pecans	3 egg yolks, beaten
3 tablespoons butter	3 egg whites, beaten
1½ cups light cream	2 cups heavy cream, lightly whipped
¾ cup granulated sugar	2 teaspoons vanilla extract
¼ teaspoon salt	

1. In a skillet, brown the pecans in the butter. Cool.
2. In a saucepan, combine light cream, sugar, and salt. Heat, stirring occasionally, to a boil. Cool.
3. Mix together beaten egg yolks, cooled pecans, cooled light cream mixture, beaten egg whites, lightly whipped heavy cream, and vanilla extract.
4. Churn-freeze.

Makes ½ gallon

Buttermilk Ice Cream

1 cup water	1 cup canned unsweetened pineapple juice
1½ cups granulated sugar	⅛ teaspoon salt
1 teaspoon finely grated lemon rind	5 cups buttermilk
1 teaspoon finely grated orange rind	

1. In a saucepan, combine water and sugar and boil for 5 minutes. Cool until lukewarm.
2. Add lemon rind, orange rind, pineapple juice, and salt to the lukewarm sugar syrup.
3. Churn-freeze until mushy.
4. Add buttermilk to the partially frozen mixture. Stir well.
5. Still-freeze.

Makes ½ gallon

Buttermint Ice Cream

1½ cups buttermints
3 cups evaporated milk
3 cups heavy cream,
   lightly whipped

⅛ teaspoon green food
   coloring

1. Press the mints with a rolling pin until well crushed.
2. Heat evaporated milk to a boil, and then pour hot milk on the crushed mints, stirring. Cool.
3. Add lightly whipped cream and green food coloring to the cooled mint mixture.
4. Churn-freeze.

Makes ½ gallon

Butterscotch Ice Cream

¼ cup butter
2 cups dark brown sugar
3½ cups milk
⅓ cup flour
¼ teaspoon salt

2 egg yolks
2 cups heavy cream
¼ teaspoon almond
   extract

1. In a saucepan, combine butter and 1½ cups of the brown sugar. Cook on low heat, stirring, until sugar melts.
2. In another saucepan, heat milk to a boil.
3. Add hot milk, stirring constantly, to the melted sugar.
4. Mix together flour, remaining ½ cup brown sugar, and salt and add this mixture to the hot milk and sugar mixture.
5. In the top of a double boiler, stirring constantly, cook combined mixture until thickened.
6. In a bowl, beat egg yolks until thick.
7. While stirring, pour hot thickened mixture into yolks.

8. Return mixture to double boiler. Cook, stirring, 3 minutes. Cool.

9. Add heavy cream and almond extract to cooled mixture.

10. Churn-freeze.

Makes ½ gallon

Butterscotch Pecan Ice Cream

1½ cups granulated sugar
2 cups milk
2½ tablespoons butter
3 egg yolks, beaten
⅛ teaspoon salt
1 teaspoon vanilla
  extract

3 egg whites, stiffly
  beaten
2 cups heavy cream
1 cup pecans, chopped

1. Caramelize ¾ cup of the sugar. (To caramelize sugar, put sugar in a heavy skillet and cook, stirring constantly, over medium heat—338° F—until sugar turns to a golden brown syrup.)

2. In the top of a double boiler, combine caramelized sugar, remaining ¾ cup sugar, milk, butter, and beaten egg yolks. Cook, stirring constantly, until thickened. Cool.

3. Add salt, vanilla, stiffly beaten egg whites, heavy cream, and chopped pecans to the cooled mixture.

4. Churn-freeze.

Makes ½ gallon

Cantaloupe Ice Cream

1 cup milk
1 cup granulated sugar
2 cups ripe cantaloupe
   pulp (about 1 medium-
   sized melon or 2 or 3
   very small melons)
⅓ cup fresh lemon juice

Few drops red and yellow
   food coloring
3 egg whites, stiffly
   beaten
2 cups heavy cream,
   lightly whipped

1. Combine milk and sugar and heat until sugar dissolves. Cool.
2. Scoop pulp from cantaloupe and blend pulp and juice into a purée.
3. Combine cantaloupe purée, lemon juice, a few drops red and yellow food coloring, the milk and sugar mixture, stiffly beaten egg whites, and lightly whipped heavy cream.
4. Churn-freeze.

Makes ½ gallon

Serve in melon half shells and top the mounded ice cream with tiny melon balls.

Caramel Ice Cream

1 cup granulated sugar
3 cups milk
¼ teaspoon salt
4 egg yolks

3 cups evaporated milk,
   whipped
1 tablespoon vanilla
   extract

1. Caramelize ⅔ cup of the sugar. (To caramelize sugar, put sugar in a heavy skillet and cook, stirring constantly, over medium heat—338° F—until sugar turns to a golden brown syrup.)

2. In top of a double boiler, heat milk to a boil.

3. Add caramelized sugar to hot milk. Cook for 5 minutes on medium heat.

4. In a bowl, add salt and remaining ⅓ cup sugar to egg yolks and beat until creamy.

5. While beating eggs vigorously, slowly add hot sugar-milk mixture to the eggs.

6. Return mixture to the top of the double boiler, and cook until thickened. Cool.

7. Add whipped evaporated milk and vanilla to the cooled mixture.

8. Churn-freeze.

Makes ½ gallon

Caramel Chocolate Ice Cream

3 ounces unsweetened
  chocolate
2 cups milk
2 egg yolks, slightly
  beaten
1 cup granulated sugar

½ cup boiling water
⅛ teaspoon salt
3 cups heavy cream,
  lightly whipped
2 teaspoons vanilla
  extract

1. In top of double boiler, heat chocolate and milk until chocolate melts.

2. Blend by beating with a wire whip or rotary beater, and while beating, add slightly beaten egg yolks. Continue to cook on medium heat for 2 minutes without stirring.

3. Melt sugar in skillet, stirring constantly. When sugar is a golden syrup, add boiling water and simmer until smooth.

4. Add sugar syrup and salt to hot chocolate mixture and mix thoroughly. Cool.

5. Fold lightly whipped heavy cream and vanilla into cooled chocolate mixture.

6. Churn-freeze.

Makes ½ gallon

Carbonated Strawberry Ice Cream

2   bottles strawberry
    soda pop (10-ounce
    size)
1   package frozen straw-
    berries (10-ounce
    size), thawed
3   eggs, beaten

½   cup granulated sugar
1½ cups sweetened
    condensed milk
1½ cups light cream
1   teaspoon vanilla
    extract

1. Stir together all ingredients, mixing well.
2. Churn-freeze.

Makes ½ gallon

Cashew Nut Ice Cream

½   pound unsalted
    cashew nuts, skinned
    and chopped
1   pound strained honey
3   egg yolks, beaten

⅛   teaspoon salt
3   egg whites, stiffly
    beaten
1½ cups heavy cream,
    lightly whipped

1. Combine cashew nuts and honey, mixing well.
2. Add beaten egg yolks, salt, stiffly beaten egg whites, and lightly whipped heavy cream to the nut-honey mixture.
3. Churn-freeze.

Makes ½ gallon

If you are using salted cashews, quickly rinse salted nuts first in boiling water and then in cold water. Pat them dry with paper towels.

Chestnut Ice Cream

1½ cups boiled fresh
   chestnuts
 5 egg yolks
1½ cups granulated sugar

3 cups milk
¼ teaspoon salt
1 cup evaporated milk
¼ cup pineapple syrup

1. Purée boiled chestnuts in an electric blender.
2. Beat together egg yolks and sugar.
3. In top of double boilcr, heat milk to a boil and, while beating eggs vigorously, slowly pour hot milk into egg mixture. Return combined mixture to the double boiler. Cook, stirring, until thickened. Cool.
4. Add chestnut purée, salt, evaporated milk, and pineapple syrup to the cooled mixture.
5. Churn-freeze.

Makes ½ gallon

Chestnuts can be shelled by slitting each shell with a sharp knife. Roast in oven for 5 minutes at medium temperature. Remove shells and then let boil in water for 20 minutes.

√ Chocolate Ice Cream I

4 ounces bitter
   chocolate
1 cup granulated sugar
1 tablespoon flour
¼ teaspoon salt

3 eggs
3 cups milk
1½ tablespoons vanilla
   extract
3 cups heavy cream

1. In top of double boiler, melt chocolate.
2. Add sugar, flour, and salt to melted chocolate.

3. Beat eggs with rotary beater, and add beaten eggs to chocolate mixture, stirring vigorously.

4. Heat milk to a boil and add to chocolate mixture. Cook, stirring occasionally, until mixture thickens. Cool.

5. Add vanilla and heavy cream to the cooled mixture.

6. Churn-freeze.

Makes ½ gallon

Chocolate Ice Cream II

½ cup granulated sugar	4 egg yolks
⅔ cup water	4 cups heavy cream,
16 ounces semisweet	whipped
chocolate pieces	

1. Heat sugar and water, allowing mixture to boil for 2 minutes.

2. Add hot sugar syrup to chocolate pieces and blend in an electric blender until smooth.

3. Add egg yolks and continue to blend until well mixed.

4. Combine whipped heavy cream and chocolate mixture.

5. Still-freeze (or churn-freeze).

Makes ½ gallon

Chocolate Chip Ice Cream

6 cups heavy cream	1 cup granulated sugar
3 tablespoons	1 tablespoon vanilla
cornstarch	extract
¾ cup milk	12 ounces semisweet
4 eggs, beaten	chocolate bits

1. In top of double boiler, heat heavy cream.
2. Dissolve cornstarch in the milk and add to the hot cream. Cook, stirring occasionally, until slightly thickened.
3. Beat a tablespoon of the hot custard into the beaten eggs and then stir eggs into custard. Continue to cook until thick. Remove from heat.
4. Add sugar to custard and beat until smooth. Cool.
5. Add vanilla and chocolate to the cooled custard.
6. Churn-freeze.

Makes ½ gallon

√ Chocolate Chip Mint Ice Cream

1 cup granulated sugar	¼ cup finely crushed
4 eggs	peppermint candy
¼ teaspoon salt	2½ cups milk
1½ cups grated milk	2 cups heavy cream
chocolate	

1. Combine sugar and eggs. Beat until creamy.
2. Add salt, grated chocolate, peppermint candy, milk, and cream to the sugar and eggs.
3. Churn-freeze.

Makes ½ gallon

Chocolate-Covered Peppermint Ice Cream

30 chocolate-covered	1 tablespoon vanilla
peppermint candies	extract
1½ cups granulated sugar	6 cups heavy cream,
¾ cup water	whipped
6 egg whites	

1. In top of double boiler, heat peppermint candies until melted.
2. In a saucepan, combine sugar and water. Boil for 5 minutes.
3. Beat egg whites with electric mixer until stiff.
4. While beating egg whites on high speed, slowly add hot sugar syrup to egg whites.
5. Add vanilla, whipped heavy cream, and melted candy to the egg white mixture. Mix well.
6. Still-freeze.

Makes ½ gallon

Chocolate Cinnamon Ice Cream

4 ounces unsweetened chocolate	2 tablespoons vanilla extract
2 cups condensed milk	¼ teaspoon salt
4 cups light cream	2 teaspoons ground cinnamon
½ cup water	

1. In top of double boiler, melt the chocolate.
2. Stir condensed milk into the melted chocolate and cook, stirring, for 5 minutes. Cool.
3. Stir light cream into chocolate mixture.
4. Add, mixing well, water, vanilla, salt, and cinnamon.
5. Churn-freeze.

Makes ½ gallon

Chocolate Fig Ice Cream

1¼ cups fresh fig purée (about 10 very small figs, or ¾ pound)	¾ cup granulated sugar
	6 ounces semisweet chocolate
¾ cup cider	3 cups heavy cream

1 teaspoon vanilla   ¼ teaspoon salt
    extract

1. Peel figs and purée in an electric blender.
2. Combine fig purée with cider. Let stand for 1 hour.
3. In top of double boiler, combine sugar and chocolate. Heat until chocolate melts. Cool.
4. Mix together fig mixture, chocolate mixture, heavy cream, vanilla, and salt.
5. Churn-freeze.

Makes ½ gallon

Chocolate Marbled Ice Cream

3 cups heavy cream   1 tablespoon vanilla
3 cups milk   extract
1 Junket rennet tablet   1 cup canned chocolate
1 tablespoon cold water   syrup
½ cup granulated sugar

1. In a saucepan, combine cream and milk. Heat until lukewarm.
2. Dissolve rennet tablet in the water.
3. Add sugar, dissolved rennet tablet, and vanilla to the lukewarm cream-milk mixture. Let stand at room temperature for 10 minutes, then chill in the refrigerator for 1 hour.
4. Churn-freeze until firm.
5. Open freezer can. Pour chocolate syrup into mixture, stirring with knife to create marble effect.

Makes ½ gallon

Chocolate Marshmallow Ice Cream

8 ounces unsweetened
chocolate
30 marshmallows
2 cups milk
2 teaspoons flour
¼ teaspoon salt

½ cup granulated sugar
1 cup heavy cream,
lightly whipped
2 cups evaporated milk
½ teaspoon fresh lemon
juice

1. In top of double boiler, melt chocolate.
2. Cut marshmallows in half (use kitchen shears).
3. Heat milk to a boil and add to melted chocolate.
4. Combine flour, salt, and sugar and then coat marshmallows with this mixture.
5. Add coated marshmallows and remaining sugar mixture to the hot milk-chocolate mixture. Cool.
6. Add lightly whipped cream, evaporated milk, and lemon juice to the cooled mixture. Mix well.
7. Still-freeze (or churn-freeze).

Makes ½ gallon

Chocolate Spice Ice Cream

2 ounces unsweetened
chocolate
3½ cups milk
1 cinnamon stick (2 to 3
inches)
¼ teaspoon ground
ginger
¼ cup cold water
¼ cup flour

1½ cups granulated sugar
4 egg yolks
1 cup heavy cream
¼ teaspoon salt
1½ teaspoons vanilla
extract
½ teaspoon almond
extract

1. In top of double boiler, melt chocolate.

2. Stirring constantly, add milk, cinnamon stick, and ground ginger to the chocolate.

3. Mix cold water and flour and add to chocolate mixture. Heat until thickened (about 20 minutes), stirring occasionally. Remove cinnamon stick.

4. Add sugar and egg yolks to the chocolate mixture. Stirring, cook 2 minutes and then remove from heat and beat with rotary beater until cool.

5. Whip heavy cream with salt.

6. Add whipped cream, vanilla, and almond extract to cooled chocolate.

7. Churn-freeze.

Makes ½ gallon

Chocolate Syrup Ice Cream

4 cups light cream	1 tablespoon cold water
½ cup canned chocolate syrup	½ teaspoon vanilla extract
¾ cup granulated sugar	2 cups heavy cream, lightly whipped
2 Junket rennet tablets	

1. Mix light cream, chocolate syrup, and sugar and heat in top of double boiler until lukewarm.

2. Dissolve junket tablets in 1 tablespoon of cold water and add to the chocolate mixture with the vanilla.

3. Remove pot from stove, allowing mixture to remain above hot water in the double boiler, until slightly thickened. Cool.

4. Fold chocolate mixture into lightly whipped heavy cream.

5. Churn-freeze.

Makes ½ gallon

Cinnamon Ice Cream

1¾ cups granulated sugar
⅓ cup water
1½ tablespoons ground
  cinnamon
3 cups light cream

1 egg yolk
1 teaspoon vanilla
2 cups heavy cream,
  lightly whipped

1. In a saucepan, mix together sugar, water, and cinnamon. Cook, stirring, until sugar dissolves. Remove from heat.
2. In top of double boiler, bring light cream to a boil.
3. While beating egg yolk, slowly pour a few tablespoons hot light cream into egg. Add egg mixture to the double boiler. Cook, stirring constantly, until thickened. Cool.
4. Add cinnamon syrup, vanilla, and lightly whipped heavy cream to the cooled egg mixture.
5. Churn-freeze.

Makes ½ gallon

Cinnamon Candy Ice Cream

1½ cups granulated sugar
¾ cup water
⅛ teaspoon salt
½ cup cinnamon candy,
  crushed

5 cups heavy cream,
  lightly whipped
2 teaspoons vanilla
  extract

1. In a saucepan, combine sugar, water, salt, and ¼ cup cinnamon candy. Let boil for 5 minutes, or until candy pieces melt. Cool.

2. Add lightly whipped heavy cream, vanilla, and remaining ¼ cup candy to the cooled cinnamon mixture.
3. Churn-freeze.

Makes ½ gallon

I use "red hots" for this ice cream.

Coconut Ice Cream I

2 cups coconut milk	2 eggs, lightly beaten
1 cup milk	⅛ teaspoon salt
1 cup granulated sugar	Meat of 2 coconuts
1 tablespoon flour	3 cups heavy cream

1. In top of double boiler, combine coconut milk and milk. Heat to a boil.
2. Add sugar, flour, lightly beaten eggs, and salt to the hot milk, stirring constantly. Cook, stirring, until thickened. Cool slightly.
3. Add meat of the coconuts to the slightly cooled custard and purée in an electric blender on high speed.
4. Add heavy cream to the coconut mixture.
5. Churn-freeze.

Makes ½ gallon

To make the coconut meat easy to remove from the shell, place the unopened coconuts in a 450° F oven for 15 minutes. Then crack the coconuts by giving them several sharp blows with a hammer, on the end without the eyes.

To prepare coconut milk, grate the meat of ½ coconut into 2 cups of hot milk and let this mixture stand for 1½ hours. Then strain the mixture through several thicknesses of cheesecloth. The resulting liquid is coconut milk.

For a perfectly smooth coconut ice cream, I strain the blended coconut mixture through a food mill and add only the resulting fine purée to the heavy cream.

Coconut Ice Cream II

1 vanilla bean (3 inches)	¼ teaspoon salt
2 cups milk	2½ cups grated fresh
4 egg yolks	coconut
¾ cup granulated sugar	2½ cups heavy cream

1. Open the vanilla bean and put the seeds and pod into the milk in a saucepan. Heat to a boil.

2. In top of double boiler, mix together egg yolks, sugar, and salt.

3. Remove the vanilla pod and add hot vanilla milk to the mixture in double boiler. Cook, stirring, until thickened. Cool.

4. Add coconut and cream to the cooled mixture.

5. Churn-freeze.

Makes ½ gallon

√ Coffee Ice Cream I

3 tablespoons instant	3 cups milk
coffee	3 eggs, beaten
1 cup granulated sugar	3 cups heavy cream
3 tablespoons flour	2 teaspoons vanilla
¼ teaspoon salt	extract

1. In a saucepan, stir together the coffee, sugar, flour, salt, and milk. Continue to stir and cook until mixture thickens.

2. While beating eggs, slowly pour in a few tablespoons of the hot mixture. Mix and then add eggs to hot mixture in saucepan. Continue to cook, stirring, for 2 minutes. Cool.

3. Add cream and vanilla to the cooled mixture.

4. Churn-freeze.

Makes ½ gallon

Coffee Ice Cream II

6 tablespoons ground
  coffee
3 cups milk
2 cups granulated sugar

⅛ teaspoon salt
2½ cups heavy cream,
  lightly whipped

1. Wrap the ground coffee securely in cheesecloth, tying with string.
2. In top of double boiler, put the coffee bag in the milk. Cook until the milk is well heated and coffee-colored. Remove the coffee bag.
3. Add sugar and salt to the hot milk. Cool.
4. Add lightly whipped heavy cream to the cooled mixture.
5. Churn-freeze.

Makes ½ gallon

Coffee Almond Ice Cream

4½ cups heavy cream
1 cup strong coffee
  liquid
6 egg yolks, beaten

1 cup granulated sugar
⅛ teaspoon salt
½ pound burnt almonds

1. In a saucepan, heat cream and coffee until almost boiling.
2. Add a few tablespoons of the hot mixture to the beaten eggs, mix, and then add eggs, sugar, and salt to hot cream-coffee mixture. Continue to cook, stirring, until thickened. Strain and cool.
3. Crush almonds and add to cooled custard.
4. Churn-freeze.

Makes ½ gallon

Coffee Bean Ice Cream

1½ cups roasted coffee   ¼ teaspoon salt
     beans   ½ teaspoon vanilla
  5 cups evaporated milk   extract
  ¾ cup granulated sugar   2 cups light cream

1. In a heavy saucepan, heat coffee beans.
2. Add evaporated milk to the hot beans. Bring to a boil. Remove from heat.
3. Add sugar to the hot mixture. Stir.
4. Cover the pan tightly with first a dishcloth and then the pan lid. Let stand 1½ hours, then strain.
5. Add salt, vanilla, and light cream to the strained coffee mixture.
6. Churn-freeze.

Makes ½ gallon

Coffee Caramel Ice Cream

1 cup granulated sugar   ¼ teaspoon salt
1 tablespoon flour   2 egg yolks, beaten
2 cups light cream   ¾ teaspoon vanilla
4 cups heavy cream   extract
½ cup strong coffee
   liquid

1. Caramelize the sugar combined with the flour. (To caramelize, put sugar and flour in a heavy skillet and cook, stirring constantly, over medium heat—338° F—until mixture turns to a golden brown syrup.) Cool.
2. In top of double boiler, combine light cream, 1 cup heavy cream, the cooled caramel, coffee, and salt. Cook, stirring occasionally, until caramel dissolves.

3. Stirring vigorously, add the beaten egg yolks to the hot cream-coffee mixture. Cook, stirring, on medium heat for 5 minutes. Strain through a sieve and cool.

4. Add vanilla and remaining heavy cream to the cooled custard. Mix well.

5. Churn-freeze.

Makes ½ gallon

Corn Flake Ice Cream

¾ cup granulated sugar
1 tablespoon cornstarch
1 cup milk
1 egg yolk, beaten
3½ cups heavy cream,
 lightly whipped

2 cups crushed corn flakes
½ teaspoon vanilla
 extract
⅛ teaspoon salt
¼ teaspoon almond
 extract

1. In top of double boiler, combine sugar, cornstarch, and milk. Cook until mixture thickens.

2. Beating vigorously, add beaten egg yolk to the hot mixture. Cook, stirring, for 3 minutes. Strain and cool.

3. Add lightly whipped heavy cream, crushed corn flakes, vanilla extract, salt, and almond extract to the cooled mixture.

4. Churn-freeze.

Makes ½ gallon

Cranberry Ice Cream

4 cups cranberry sauce
⅓ cup fresh orange juice
⅓ cup fresh lemon juice

⅛ teaspoon salt
3 cups heavy cream,
 lightly whipped

1. Combine cranberry sauce, orange juice, lemon juice, salt, and lightly whipped heavy cream.
2. Churn-freeze.

Makes ½ gallon

Crunchy Lemon Ice Cream

4 cups heavy cream, whipped	¾ cup corn flakes, crushed
2 cups frozen concentrated lemonade	¾ cup pecans, finely chopped
1 cup granulated sugar	½ cup dark brown sugar
⅛ teaspoon salt	
4 tablespoons butter, melted	

1. Mix together whipped heavy cream, lemonade, sugar, and salt.
2. In a separate bowl, mix together melted butter, crushed corn flakes, chopped pecans, and brown sugar.
3. Pour the lemon-cream mixture into freezing container. Then lightly swirl the corn flake-pecan mixture through the lemon cream.
4. Still-freeze.

Makes ½ gallon

Cucumber Ice Cream

2 cups cucumber pulp and juice (about 1 very large cucumber, or 1 pound)	5 cups heavy cream, lightly whipped
	¾ cup granulated sugar
	¾ teaspoon salt

1. Peel cucumber, slice in half, remove seeds, and then chop into small pieces.

2. Purée chopped cucumber in an electric blender on medium speed.

3. Combine cucumber purée, lightly whipped cream, sugar, and salt.

4. Churn-freeze.

Makes ½ gallon

This refreshing ice cream should be served with the main course in place of a vegetable. It is fun to carve out small cucumber boats for individual serving dishes, and this also keeps the ice cream from melting if it is placed near a warm entrée.

Curaçao Ice Cream

1½ cups granulated sugar
4½ cups heavy cream
½ cup curaçao
¾ cup fresh orange juice

2 tablespoons orange
flower water (see
page 46)

1. In top of double boiler, combine sugar and 2 cups of the heavy cream. Heat to a boil and remove from stove. Cool.
2. Add curaçao, orange juice, orange flower water, and remaining cream to the cooled mixture.
3. Churn-freeze.

Makes ½ gallon

Currant Jelly Ice Cream

6 egg whites
2 cups tart currant jelly
1½ tablespoons fresh
lemon juice

4 cups heavy cream

1. Stiffly beat the egg whites.
2. Add jelly slowly to the egg whites, beating as jelly is added.
3. Add lemon juice and whipped heavy cream to the egg white–jelly mixture. Mix well.
4. Still-freeze.

Makes ½ gallon

Date Ice Cream

4 eggs	1 tablespoon vanilla
¼ teaspoon salt	extract
3 cups milk	1 cup chopped dates
¾ cup granulated sugar	⅓ cup ginger syrup
2 cups heavy cream,	
lightly whipped	

1. Combine eggs and salt. Beat until creamy with a rotary beater.
2. In top of double boiler, heat milk to a boil.
3. While stirring vigorously, slowly pour hot milk into beaten eggs. Mix well and then return mixture to top of double boiler. Cook, stirring, until thickened. Cool and strain through a sieve.
4. Add sugar, lightly whipped heavy cream, vanilla, chopped dates, and ginger syrup to the cooled mixture.
5. Churn-freeze.

Makes ½ gallon

Ginger syrup can be obtained from a jar of preserved ginger. This ice cream is also good when figs are used in place of dates.

Diabetic Vanilla Ice Cream

3 tablespoons gelatin	1 tablespoon vanilla
¾ cup cold water	extract
1½ cups boiling water	¼ teaspoon salt
4 cups milk	3 grains saccharin
4 egg yolks, beaten	4 egg whites, beaten

1. Soften gelatin in the cold water.
2. In top of double boiler, combine boiling water, milk,

and softened gelatin. Cook, stirring, on medium heat until gelatin is dissolved.

3. While beating egg yolks vigorously, add ½ cup of the hot gelatin mixture to the egg yolks. Then beat egg yolk mixture into the milk-gelatin mixture in top of double boiler. Cook, stirring, until slightly thickened. Cool.

4. Add vanilla, salt, saccharin, and beaten egg whites to cooled mixture. Mix well.

5. Still-freeze.

Makes ½ gallon

Eggnog Ice Cream

2½ cups milk
1½ teaspoons ground nutmeg
8 egg yolks
1 cup granulated sugar
⅛ teaspoon salt
½ cup dry or sweet sherry
2½ cups heavy cream, lightly whipped

1. In top of double boiler, combine milk and nutmeg. Cook until milk is hot.

2. Beat egg yolks, sugar, and salt together and slowly beat into hot milk. Continue to cook until mixture thickens. Cool.

3. Add sherry and lightly whipped cream to the cooled mixture.

4. Churn-freeze.

Makes ½ gallon

English Toffee Ice Cream

64 marshmallows (1 pound)
3 cups milk
1½ cups heavy cream
1 cup English toffee, finely crushed

1. In a saucepan, combine marshmallows with ½ cup milk. Heat, rotating marshmallows, until almost melted. Remove from the stove, continuing to stir marshmallows until they are smooth and slightly cooled.
2. Add remaining milk, heavy cream, and finely crushed toffee to the marshmallows.
3. Churn-freeze.

Makes ½ gallon

Fig Ice Cream I

½ cup milk
2 egg yolks, beaten
1½ cups heavy cream
1 quart fresh figs
1 tablespoon fresh
    lemon juice

½ cup granulated sugar
1 teaspoon vanilla ex-
    tract

1. In top of double boiler, heat milk to a boil.
2. Beating vigorously, add beaten egg yolks to the hot milk. Cook mixture until thickened. Cool.
3. Whip heavy cream and fold it into the cooled custard.
4. Peel figs and purée in an electric blender, with the lemon juice, sugar, and vanilla.
5. Add fig purée mixture to the custard-cream mixture.
6. Churn-freeze.

Makes ½ gallon

Fig Ice Cream II

1½ cups evaporated milk
1½ cups water
5 egg yolks, beaten
1 cup granulated sugar
¾ teaspoon salt
1 pound dried figs,
    ground

1 tablespoon vanilla
    extract
5 egg whites, stiffly
    beaten
1½ cups heavy cream

1. In top of double boiler, mix together evaporated milk and water. Heat to a boil.

2. While beating vigorously, slowly add beaten egg yolks and sugar to the hot milk. Cook, stirring, until thickened. Cool.

3. Add salt, ground dried figs, vanilla, stiffly beaten egg whites, and heavy cream to the cooled mixture.

4. Churn-freeze.

Makes ½ gallon

Ginger Ice Cream

2   tablespoons flour
⅛ teaspoon salt
1   cup granulated sugar
2   cups milk
3   cups heavy cream

2   egg yolks
⅔ cup preserved ginger, chopped
1½ teaspoons vanilla extract

1. In top of double boiler, mix together flour, salt, sugar, milk, and 1 cup of the heavy cream. Cook, stirring, until hot and well blended.

2. Beat egg yolks until creamy, then, while stirring vigorously, add a few tablespoons of the hot mixture to the egg yolks. Then add egg yolks and chopped ginger to the hot mixture. Let stand for 5 minutes. Strain through a sieve and cool.

3. Lightly whip remaining 2 cups of heavy cream and add with vanilla extract to the cooled mixture.

4. Churn-freeze.

Makes ½ gallon

Gooseberry Ice Cream

3 cups fresh goose-
   berries
2 cups granulated sugar
¾ cup water
¼ teaspoon green food
   coloring

2 cups heavy cream
2 teaspoons brandy
   (optional)

1. In a saucepan, combine gooseberries, sugar, and water. Cook, stirring occasionally, on low heat, until gooseberries are soft.
2. Strain the gooseberry mixture through a fine sieve. Press through as much gooseberry pulp as possible. Cool.
3. Add green food coloring, heavy cream, and brandy to the gooseberries.
4. Churn-freeze.

Makes ½ gallon

Graham Cracker Ice Cream

2 cups crushed graham
   crackers
1 cup granulated sugar
5 cups heavy cream,
   lightly whipped

1½ teaspoons vanilla
    extract

1. Mix together crushed graham crackers, sugar, lightly whipped heavy cream, and vanilla.
2. Churn-freeze.

Makes ½ gallon

Grand Marnier Ice Cream I

4½ cups heavy cream   ¼ cup Grand Marnier
 2 cups frozen concen-
    trated orange juice

1. Whip heavy cream.
2. Combine frozen orange juice with Grand Marnier.
3. Stir cream into slightly thawed orange juice-Grand Marnier mixture.
4. Still-freeze.

Makes ½ gallon

Grand Marnier Ice Cream II

 2 cups granulated sugar   ½ cup Grand Marnier
 ¾ cup water   2½ cups heavy cream,
 8 egg yolks   lightly whipped

1. In a saucepan, combine sugar and water. Boil for 5 minutes.
2. Beat egg yolks until creamy, and while beating, gradually add sugar syrup.
3. Cook combined mixture on medium heat, stirring, until thickened. Cool and strain.
4. Add Grand Marnier and lightly whipped cream to the cooled mixture.
5. Churn-freeze.

Makes ½ gallon

Grape Ice Cream I

3 pounds fresh Concord   ⅛ teaspoon salt
   grapes   2 cups heavy cream
1¼ cups granulated sugar

1. Heat grapes over low flame, stirring and pressing grapes with a spoon to separate skins and seeds from the pulp.

2. Mix sugar and salt into the grapes and continue to cook on low heat for 10 minutes, stirring occasionally. Strain and cool.

3. Lightly whip cream and stir into grape mixture.

4. Churn-freeze.

Makes ½ gallon

Grape Ice Cream II

2⅔ cups sweetened con-
    densed milk
2 cups canned or fresh
    grape juice

¼ teaspoon salt
¼ teaspoon lemon
    extract
4 cups heavy cream

1. Mix together condensed milk, grape juice, salt, and lemon extract.
2. Lightly whip heavy cream and fold it into grape juice mixture.
3. Churn-freeze.

Makes ½ gallon

If you are near a vineyard, I like the suggestion of an 1888 author for grape ice cream. He recommended the cook find the "sprightliest and richest in flavor grapes that can be had, that they be mashed without bruising the seeds, strained and the juice mixed with the proper ingredients." If grape picking is not convenient, canned grape juice is excellent in this ice cream too.

Grape Nut Ice Cream

2 cups milk
½ cup granulated sugar
4 egg yolks, beaten
⅛ teaspoon salt

3 cups heavy cream
2 teaspoons almond
    extract
1 cup grape nuts

1. In top of double boiler, heat milk to a boil.
2. Combine sugar, egg yolks, and salt. Beat with rotary beater, adding small amount of hot milk while beating. Then add yolks to hot milk in the double boiler. Cook, stirring, until mixture thickens. Cool and strain through a sieve.

3. Add heavy cream, almond extract, and grape nuts to the cooled mixture.
4. Churn-freeze.

Makes ½ gallon

Grapefruit Ice Cream

4 grapefruits
4 cups heavy cream
2¾ cups granulated sugar
2 ounces Cointreau
(optional)
Juice of 2 lemons

1. Cut and squeeze grapefruits, reserving pulp and juice.
2. Combine pulp, juice, heavy cream, sugar, Cointreau, and juice of the lemons.
3. Churn-freeze.

Makes ½ gallon

Grated Apple Ice Cream

3½ cups heavy cream
3 cups raw apple, grated
1 cup granulated sugar
⅓ cup fresh lemon juice
⅛ teaspoon salt

1. Combine cream, apple, sugar, lemon juice, and salt.
2. Churn-freeze.

Makes ½ gallon

Greengage Plum Ice Cream

2 cups peeled, stoned, and chopped fresh greengage plums
1 cup granulated sugar
½ cup water
¾ cup canned grape juice
2½ cups heavy cream, lightly whipped

1. In a saucepan, combine greengages, sugar, and water. Cook on low heat until greengages are tender. Cool.

2. Add grape juice to greengage mixture and press combined mixture through a sieve.

3. Combine lightly whipped heavy cream and greengage mixture.

4. Churn-freeze.

Makes ½ gallon

Hazelnut Ice Cream

¾ pound hazelnuts, ground	1¼ cups granulated sugar
2½ cups milk	3 egg yolks
½ cup boiling water	¼ teaspoon vanilla extract

1. In a saucepan, cover hazelnuts with water and boil for 30 minutes.

2. In an electric blender, combine drained nuts and milk. Blend on medium speed.

3. Beat together boiling water, sugar, and egg yolks and add to nut-milk mixture.

4. Stir vanilla into combined mixture.

5. Churn-freeze.

Makes ½ gallon

Hazelnuts may also be known as cobnuts or filberts.

Hokey Pokey Ice Cream

4 tablespoons un-flavored gelatin	1½ cups granulated sugar
5½ cups milk	¼ teaspoon finely grated lemon rind
4 eggs	⅛ teaspoon salt

1. Soften gelatin in 1 cup of the milk.
2. In a saucepan, mix together remaining 4½ cups milk, the eggs, sugar, lemon rind, and salt. Cook, stirring, on medium heat until slightly thickened. Remove from heat.
3. Add gelatin-milk mixture to the hot mixture. Mix well. Cool.
4. Churn-freeze.

Makes ½ gallon

Hokey Pokey was one of the earliest ice cream confections popular in England and America in the early 1900s and was sold from pushcarts for a penny a spoonful. An extra amount of gelatin was used to help it hold its texture despite peddling conditions.

Honey Almond Ice Cream

5 cups evaporated milk	2 teaspoons almond extract
1½ cups light honey	
1 tablespoon grated orange rind	1⅓ cups toasted almonds, chopped
¼ teaspoon salt	

1. Chill evaporated milk in the refrigerator.
2. Beat chilled milk with rotary beater, gradually adding honey, orange rind, salt, and almond extract.
3. Stir chopped toasted almonds into the mixture. (To toast almonds, place in a frying pan and cook, stirring continuously, on medium heat for 5 minutes.)
4. Churn-freeze.

Makes ½ gallon

Honey and Black Walnut Ice Cream

3 egg yolks, beaten
1 cup honey
2 cups milk
1 cup water
⅛ teaspoon salt

1 teaspoon walnut
   flavoring
2 cups heavy cream
1 cup chopped black
   walnuts

1. In top of double boiler, mix together egg yolks, honey, milk, water, and salt. Cook, stirring, until slightly thickened. Cool.

2. Add walnut flavoring, heavy cream, and black walnuts to the cooled mixture.

3. Churn-freeze.

Makes ½ gallon

Honey Date Ice Cream

6 egg yolks
1¼ cups honey
2 cups milk
2 cups heavy cream,
   lightly whipped

½ cup finely chopped
  dates
1 teaspoon vanilla
   extract

1. In bowl of an electric mixer, combine egg yolks and honey. Beat on medium speed until well blended.

2. In top of double boiler, heat milk to a boil.

3. While beating on medium speed, slowly add hot milk to the egg-honey mixture.

4. Return milk, egg, and honey mixture to the top of the double boiler. Cook, stirring, until thickened. Cool.

5. Add lightly whipped heavy cream, chopped dates, and vanilla to the cooled mixture.

6. Churn-freeze.

Makes ½ gallon

√ Indiana Persimmon Ice Cream

⅔ cup persimmon pulp
   (about 20 per-
   simmons, or 1 pint)
1¾ cups granulated sugar
1½ tablespoons flour
4 eggs

⅛ teaspoon salt
1½ cups heavy cream
2 tablespoons fresh
   lemon juice
3½ cups milk

1. Remove seeds from the persimmons, but do not skin. Purée persimmons in an electric blender on medium speed.

2. Combine sugar, flour, eggs, salt, cream, persimmon pulp, lemon juice, and milk. Beat with wire whip until well blended.

3. Churn-freeze.   *Makes ½ gallon*

This old Hoosier dessert, made with the tiny persimmons

of the Midwest, is a treat I wish the whole world could share. It is traditionally served at the Parke County Covered Bridge Festival in Rockville, Indiana. This festival is held in October when the fall foliage, persimmons, bittersweet, and cider are at their best.

✓ Lemon Ice Cream

2 cups granulated sugar
¼ cup fresh lemon juice
1 tablespoon grated lemon rind

5 cups heavy cream
¼ teaspoon yellow food coloring

1. Combine sugar, lemon juice, and lemon rind.
2. Whip cream lightly and add it to lemon mixture.
3. Add yellow food coloring. Mix well.
4. Still-freeze (or churn-freeze).

Makes ½ gallon

This is a jewel of a cream because it can be frozen without stirring, which makes it perfect for pouring directly into lemon shells and freezing in the refrigerator freezer. The shell gives the ice cream a tangier flavor.

Lemon Drop Ice Cream

2 cups granulated sugar
4 teaspoons finely grated lemon peel
¼ cup fresh lemon juice
3 cups evaporated milk

4 drops yellow food coloring
1 cup crushed lemon drop candy

1. Mix together sugar, lemon peel, lemon juice, evaporated milk, food coloring, and crushed lemon drop candy.
2. Churn-freeze.

Makes ½ gallon

Lemon Mint Ice Cream

¾ cup chopped fresh
    mint
½ cup granulated sugar
4 eggs
1¼ cups light corn syrup
1 cup light cream

3 cups milk
⅛ teaspoon salt
½ cup fresh lemon juice
2 teaspoons grated
    lemon rind

1. Combine mint and sugar by pressing mixture with a rolling pin.
2. Combine eggs and corn syrup and beat with rotary beater.
3. Add to the egg–corn syrup mixture, mixing well, the mint and sugar mixture, light cream, milk, salt, lemon juice, and lemon rind.
4. Churn-freeze.

Makes ½ gallon

Lemon Walnut Ice Cream

4 eggs, beaten
1 cup granulated sugar
1 cup light corn syrup
1 tablespoon grated
    lemon rind

½ cup fresh lemon juice
4 cups light cream
¾ cup black walnuts,
    chopped

1. Combine beaten eggs and sugar. Beat until thick.
2. Add, mixing thoroughly, corn syrup, lemon rind, lemon juice, light cream, and walnuts to the egg-sugar mixture.
3. Churn-freeze.

Makes ½ gallon

Lime Ice Cream

4 eggs
1 cup granulated sugar
1 cup light corn syrup
½ cup fresh lime juice
2 teaspoons finely
grated lime rind

¼ teaspoon green food
coloring
2 cups light cream,
lightly whipped
3 cups heavy cream,
lightly whipped

1. Combine eggs and sugar. Beat with rotary beater.
2. Add corn syrup, lime juice, lime rind, food coloring, and lightly whipped light and heavy cream to the egg-sugar mixture. Mix well.
3. Churn-freeze.

Makes ½ gallon

Lime Orange Ice Cream

1½ cups milk
4 eggs, beaten
½ cup granulated sugar
⅛ teaspoon salt
2 tablespoons un-
flavored gelatin
2 cups fresh orange juice

½ cup fresh lime juice
1¼ cups light corn syrup
2 cups light cream
1 tablespoon grated
orange rind
1 tablespoon grated
lemon rind

1. In top of double boiler, combine milk, beaten eggs, sugar, and salt. Cook, stirring constantly, for 6 minutes.
2. Dissolve gelatin in orange juice, for 5 minutes.
3. Stir orange-gelatin, lime juice, and corn syrup into warm milk mixture. Cool.
4. Fold cream, orange rind, and lemon rind into cooled mixture.
5. Churn-freeze.

Makes ½ gallon

Macaroon Ice Cream

2 cups macaroon
crumbs
1 cup confectioners'
sugar

5 cups heavy cream
1 teaspoon almond
extract
⅛ teaspoon salt

1. Combine and mix well macaroon crumbs, sugar, cream, almond extract, and salt.
2. Churn-freeze.

Makes ½ gallon

Macaroon Maple Ice Cream

1 cup maple syrup
6 egg yolks
2 cups macaroon
crumbs
⅛ teaspoon salt

4 cups heavy cream,
lightly whipped
¼ teaspoon vanilla
extract

1. In top of double boiler, heat maple syrup until very hot but not boiling.
2. Beat egg yolks until creamy.
3. While beating eggs vigorously, slowly add hot syrup to the eggs. Return mixture to top of double boiler. Cook, stirring, until thickened.
4. Add macaroon crumbs and salt to the hot mixture. Cool.
5. Add lightly whipped heavy cream and vanilla extract to the cooled mixture.
6. Churn-freeze.

Makes ½ gallon

Mango Ice Cream

2 cups fresh mango
   purée (about 2
   medium-size mangoes,
   or 1¾ pounds)
1 cup granulated sugar
⅛ teaspoon cream of
   tartar

⅓ cup water
Juice of 1 lime
4 cups heavy cream,
   lightly whipped

1. Purée mangoes in an electric blender on medium speed, or mash with wooden potato masher.
2. In a saucepan, mix together sugar, cream of tartar, and water. Boil for 5 minutes, stirring occasionally. Cool.
3. Combine mango purée, juice of the lime, lightly whipped heavy cream, and cooled sugar syrup.
4. Churn-freeze.

Makes ½ gallon

Maple Coffee Ice Cream

1½ cups milk
1½ cups maple syrup
 4 egg yolks, beaten
 ¼ teaspoon salt

2½ cups strong coffee
   liquid
1½ cups heavy cream,
   lightly whipped

1. In a saucepan, heat the milk and maple syrup to boil. Beat with a rotary beater until well mixed. Cool.
2. Combine beaten egg yolks and salt and add to the cooled mixture.
3. In a double boiler, cook combined mixture until thickened. Remove from heat.
4. Add coffee. Cool.
5. Fold in lightly whipped cream.
6. Churn-freeze.

Makes ½ gallon

Maple Sugar Ice Cream

3 cups milk	3 cups heavy cream
1½ cups maple sugar	1 tablespoon vanilla
¼ cup flour	extract
2 eggs, beaten	⅛ teaspoon salt

1. In top of double boiler, combine milk and 1 cup of the maple sugar, the flour, and beaten eggs. Mix well. Cook, stirring occasionally, for 25 minutes. Cool.

2. Add heavy cream, vanilla, salt, and remaining maple sugar to the cooled mixture.

3. Churn-freeze.

Makes ½ gallon

Maple Walnut Ice Cream

2 cups maple syrup	4 egg whites, stiffly
4 egg yolks, beaten	beaten
¼ cup confectioners'	2 cups heavy cream,
sugar	lightly whipped
2 teaspoons vanilla	2 cups walnuts, chopped
extract	

1. In top of double boiler, heat maple syrup until hot. Do not bring to boil.

2. Stirring vigorously, add egg yolks to the hot syrup. Cook until thickened. Cool.

3. Add confectioners' sugar, vanilla, stiffly beaten egg whites, lightly whipped heavy cream, and walnuts to the cooled mixture.

4. Churn-freeze.

Makes ½ gallon

Maraschino Cherry Ice Cream

2 eggs
½ cup granulated sugar
¼ cup powdered milk
1 cup condensed milk
5 cups homogenized
  milk

1 jar maraschino cher-
  ries (8-ounce size),
  undrained

1. Separate egg whites from the yolks and beat each until fluffy.
2. Stir sugar, powdered milk, condensed milk, and homogenized milk into egg yolks. Mix well.
3. Chop cherries and add with juice to egg yolk mixture.
4. Fold in the egg whites.
5. Churn-freeze.

Makes ½ gallon

Maraschino cherries are sweet red cherries soaked in a syrup of sugar, water, and oil of bitter almonds. They impart their own special flavor to this ice cream. Green-colored maraschino cherries, flavored with mint, may be substituted for the red. Top each serving with a red and a green cherry and it makes a festive holiday dessert.

Maraschino Liqueur Ice Cream

10 egg yolks
1½ cups granulated sugar
½ teaspoon salt

4 cups light cream
½ cup maraschino liqueur

1. Beat egg yolks until thick and creamy.
2. Add sugar and salt to the egg yolks, mixing well.
3. In top of double boiler, heat cream to a boil, and then, while beating eggs vigorously, slowly add hot cream to the egg mixture.

4. Return combined mixture to the top of the double boiler. Cook, stirring, until thickened. Strain and cool.
5. Add maraschino liqueur to the cooled mixture.
6. Churn-freeze.

Makes ½ gallon

Marshmallow Ice Cream

2 cups milk
30 marshmallows
¼ teaspoon salt
1 tablespoon vanilla
    extract

3 cups heavy cream,
    lightly whipped

1. In top of double boiler, combine milk and marshmallows and heat until blended. Cool.
2. Stir salt, vanilla, and lightly whipped heavy cream into cooled mixture.
3. Churn-freeze.

Makes ½ gallon

Marshmallow Mocha Ice Cream

20 marshmallows
 2 cups semisweet
     chocolate chips
 4 egg yolks

1 cup strong coffee
    liquid
3 cups heavy cream,
    whipped

1. In top of double boiler, combine marshmallows and chocolate chips. Heat until mixture melts.
2. In bowl of electric mixer, beat egg yolks until thick and creamy.
3. While beating on medium speed, add chocolate-marshmallow mixture and coffee to the egg yolks.
4. Stir whipped heavy cream into mixture.
5. Still-freeze.

Makes ½ gallon

Meringue Ice Cream

12 egg whites
¼ teaspoon salt
1 cup granulated sugar
4 cups heavy cream,
   whipped

1 tablespoon vanilla
   extract

1. Beat egg whites with salt until peaks form.
2. Slowly add sugar to egg whites. Continue to beat until well combined.
3. Fold whipped heavy cream and vanilla into egg whites.
4. Still-freeze.

Makes ½ gallon

Mocha Ice Cream

4 ounces unsweetened
   chocolate
2 cups condensed milk
2 cups evaporated milk
2 cups strong coffee
   liquid

¼ teaspoon salt
1 teaspoon vanilla
   extract
½ teaspoon ground
   cinnamon

1. In top of double boiler, melt chocolate.
2. Heat condensed milk and then add to the melted chocolate. Cook, stirring, until mixture blends. Cool.
3. Add evaporated milk, coffee, salt, vanilla, and cinnamon to the cooled mixture.
4. Churn-freeze.

Makes ½ gallon

Mocha Pecan Ice Cream

1 tablespoon unflavored gelatin	¾ cup granulated sugar
¼ cup milk	¼ teaspoon salt
1¼ cups hot strong coffee liquid	2 cups light cream
2 ounces unsweetened chocolate	1 teaspoon vanilla extract
6 tablespoons light corn syrup	2 cups heavy cream
	½ cup chopped pecans

1. Soften gelatin in milk.
2. Add gelatin mixture to hot coffee.
3. In top of double boiler, melt chocolate.
4. Add coffee mixture, corn syrup, and sugar to melted chocolate.
5. Add salt, light cream, vanilla, heavy cream, and pecans.
6. Churn-freeze.

Makes ½ gallon

Molasses Ice Cream

1¼ cups molasses	1 cup cold water
5 cups light cream	⅛ teaspoon salt

1. Combine all ingredients, mixing well.
2. Churn-freeze.

Makes ½ gallon

Nesselrode Pudding Ice Cream

10 chestnuts, roasted
 3 tablespoons mara-
    schino liqueur
 ¼ cup seedless raisins
 ¾ cup puréed boiled
    chestnuts (about 14
    chestnuts)
1½ cups milk
 ¾ cup granulated sugar
 ¼ teaspoon salt
 3 egg yolks, beaten
1½ cups light cream
 ½ cup heavy cream
 ½ cup evaporated milk
 ¼ cup canned un-
    sweetened pineapple
    juice
 ½ cup candied fruits

1. Roast and remove shells from the 10 chestnuts. Then cook roasted chestnuts for 10 minutes in boiling water. Drain. Roughly break up chestnuts. Combine chestnuts and maraschino liqueur. Let stand for 2 hours.

2. Pour boiling water on raisins and let soak for 15 minutes. Drain.

3. Purée boiled chestnuts in electric blender on medium speed.

4. In top of double boiler, heat milk, sugar, and salt.

5. While beating vigorously, add beaten egg yolks to the hot milk mixture. Cook until thickened. Strain and cool.

6. Add light cream, heavy cream, evaporated milk, pineapple juice, and puréed boiled chestnuts (do not add 10 roasted maraschino-soaked chestnuts now) to cooled custard.

7. Churn-freeze.

8. Add candied fruits, the soaked, drained raisins, and maraschino-soaked chestnuts to the ice cream as soon as the freezer is opened.

Makes ½ gallon

Nougat Ice Cream

5 egg yolks
1 cup granulated sugar
½ teaspoon salt
3 cups milk
5 egg whites
1½ cups heavy cream,
   lightly whipped
1 teaspoon almond
   extract
1¾ teaspoons vanilla
   extract
¼ cup blanched al-
   monds, chopped
¼ cup hazelnuts,
   chopped
¼ cup pistachio nuts,
   chopped
¼ cup walnuts, chopped

1. Beat together egg yolks, sugar, and salt.
2. In top of double boiler, heat milk to a boil and while beating eggs vigorously, slowly pour hot milk into egg yolk mixture. Return combined mixture to the double boiler. Cook, stirring, until thickened. Strain and cool.
3. Beat egg whites until stiff.
4. Fold egg whites, lightly whipped cream, almond and vanilla extracts, and all the chopped nuts into the cooled mixture.
5. Churn-freeze.

Makes ½ gallon

Orange Ice Cream I

1 cup fresh orange juice
1 teaspoon finely grated
   orange peel
½ cup fresh lemon juice
½ cup finely grated
   lemon peel
2 cups granulated sugar
2 cups milk
2 cups heavy cream
⅛ teaspoon salt

1. Combine all ingredients. Mix well.
2. Churn-freeze.

Makes ½ gallon

Orange Ice Cream II

2 cups heavy cream	⅛ teaspoon salt
1½ cups evaporated milk	⅔ cup granulated sugar
4 cups fresh orange juice	

1. Mix together cream, evaporated milk, orange juice, salt, and sugar.
2. Churn-freeze.

Makes ½ gallon

Orange Ice Cream III

1½ cups milk	¼ teaspoon salt
6 egg yolks	1½ cups light cream
¾ cup granulated sugar	2½ cups fresh orange juice
¾ cup light corn syrup	

1. In top of double boiler, heat milk to a boil.
2. Beat egg yolks, adding small amount of hot milk as you beat. Then add beaten egg yolks to hot milk.
3. Add sugar, corn syrup, and salt to hot milk-egg mixture. Cook, stirring, until slightly thickened. Cool.
4. Add cream and orange juice to the cooled mixture.
5. Churn-freeze.

Makes ½ gallon

Orange Ice Cream IV

3 cups milk	2 eggs, beaten
2 tablespoons flour	2 cups heavy cream
1¼ cups granulated sugar	1 cup frozen concen-
⅛ teaspoon salt	trated orange juice

1. In top of double boiler, heat milk to a boil.
2. Combine flour, sugar, salt, and beaten eggs. Mix well.
3. Slowly add, while stirring vigorously, a little hot milk to the egg mixture. Then add the egg mixture to the hot milk mixture in the double boiler. Cook, stirring, until thickened. Cool.
4. Add heavy cream and concentrated orange juice to the cooled mixture.
5. Churn-freeze.

Makes ½ gallon

Orange Yogurt Ice Cream

2 cups frozen con-	⅛ teaspoon salt
centrated orange juice	4 cups orange yogurt
1½ cups granulated sugar	4 egg whites, beaten

1. In an electric blender, combine concentrated orange juice, sugar, salt, and yogurt. Mix on medium speed until well blended.
2. Still-freeze to mush.
3. Add beaten egg whites. Mix well.
4. Still-freeze till firm.

Makes ½ gallon

√ Peach Ice Cream I

2 eggs	2 cups heavy cream
1 cup granulated sugar	2 cups milk
1 tablespoon vanilla	2 cups peeled, pitted,
extract	and mashed fresh,
½ cup condensed milk	very ripe peaches

1. Beat eggs and sugar together until very creamy.
2. Add vanilla, condensed milk, heavy cream, and milk.

3. Churn-freeze to a mush.
4. Add peaches and continue to churn-freeze till firm.

Makes ½ gallon

During our honeymoon, my husband described this delicacy of his childhood. Homemade ice cream was synonymous with the blend of peaches and cream that his Texas neighbors, the Taylor Dabneys, served. Mrs. Dabney kindly gave this recipe to me and to my delight, my husband and his brother were equally filled with nostalgia on tasting it.

Peach Ice Cream II

3 cups canned peaches
2 tablespoons unflavored gelatin
1 cup granulated sugar
¼ teaspoon salt
1 teaspoon almond extract
1 teaspoon vanilla extract
¼ teaspoon red food coloring
3 cups heavy cream, lightly whipped

1. Drain the peaches and then purée them in an electric blender.
2. Add gelatin to ¼ cup of the peach purée. Let stand for 5 minutes.
3. In a saucepan, combine remaining peach purée, sugar, and salt. Heat to a boil, stirring occasionally.
4. Add the gelatin–peach purée mixture to the hot peach mixture. Stir and cool.
5. Add almond and vanilla extracts, food coloring, and lightly whipped cream to the cooled mixture.
6. Churn-freeze.

Makes ½ gallon

The touch of red food coloring gives the fresh peach look.

Peach Ice Cream III

15 fresh ripe peaches,   1½ cups granulated sugar
    peeled and pitted   ¼ cup fresh lime juice
 3 cups sour cream

1. Purée peeled and pitted peaches in an electric blender.
2. Mix together the puréed peaches, sour cream, sugar, and lime juice.
3. Churn-freeze.

Makes ½ gallon

Peach and Banana Sour Cream Ice Cream

10 peaches, pitted   1 cup granulated sugar
 4 bananas   Juice of 2 lemons
 2 cups sour cream

1. Peel peaches and bananas, and purée in an electric blender.
2. Combine fruit purée, sour crcam, sugar, and juice of the lemons.
3. Churn-freeze.

Makes ½ gallon

Peach, Cherry, and Pecan Ice Cream

¾ cup granulated sugar   ¼ teaspoon vanilla
1 tablespoon flour   extract
⅛ teaspoon salt   15 marshmallows, cut
1½ cups milk   into small pieces
3 eggs   ½ cup finely chopped
1½ cups canned peaches,   pecans
    drained and mashed

½ cup chopped   3 cups heavy cream,
    maraschino cherries   lightly whipped

1. In top of double boiler, mix together sugar, flour, salt, and milk. Cook, stirring, for 15 minutes.
2. Beat eggs with rotary beater or wire whip.
3. Continue to beat eggs and pour hot flour-milk mixture into the eggs. Return mixture to the double boiler and cook, stirring, for 3 minutes. Cool.
4. Add peaches, vanilla, marshmallows, pecans, cherries, and lightly whipped heavy cream to the cooled mixture.
5. Churn-freeze.

Makes ½ gallon

Peach Jam Ice Cream

2¼ cups peach jam   ⅛ teaspoon salt
1½ cups evaporated milk   3 cups heavy cream,
 ¾ teaspoon almond   lightly whipped
    extract

1. Combine jam, evaporated milk, almond extract, salt, and lightly whipped heavy cream.
2. Churn-freeze.

Makes ½ gallon

Peanut Ice Cream

2 cups light cream   1½ cups finely chopped
½ cup granulated sugar   salted peanuts
3 egg yolks   2½ cups heavy cream

1. In top of double boiler, combine light cream and sugar. Heat until lukewarm.

2. Beat egg yolks until thick and creamy.

3. While beating eggs vigorously, slowly add warm cream mixture to the eggs, then return combined mixture to top of double boiler. Cook, stirring, until thickened. Cool.

4. Add finely chopped peanuts and the heavy cream to the cooled mixture.

5. Churn-freeze.

Makes ½ gallon

Peanut Brittle Ice Cream

1 tablespoon unflavored gelatin
2 tablespoons cold water
1 cup ground peanut brittle candy
2 cups milk

⅛ teaspoon salt
4 eggs, beaten
1 tablespoon vanilla extract
2½ cups heavy cream, lightly whipped

1. Dissolve gelatin in water, for 5 minutes.

2. In top of double boiler, combine ground peanut brittle, milk, and salt. Cook for 3 minutes.

3. Pour gelatin over the beaten eggs and, stirring, add gelatin-egg mixture to peanut brittle mixture. Remove from heat and cool.

4. Stir vanilla and lightly whipped cream into cooled mixture.

5. Churn-freeze.

Makes ½ gallon

Peanut Brittle Harris Ice Cream

2 cups crushed peanut
  brittle candy
5 cups heavy cream

⅛ teaspoon salt
1 tablespoon vanilla
  extract

1. Mix together peanut brittle, heavy cream, salt, and vanilla.
2. Churn-freeze.

Makes ½ gallon

My Aunt Wilma, a master at many foods, makes great peanut brittle, which is delicious by itself or in this ice cream. To make the peanut brittle, combine in a saucepan *2 cups sugar, 1 cup white corn syrup,* and *1 cup water.* Bring the mixture to a boil and then add *2 cups raw, shelled peanuts.* Cook until peanuts begin to pop. Remove from heat. Add *1 teaspoon vanilla extract* and *1 teaspoon baking soda.* Mix well. Pour mixture into a greased dish for a short time, and then onto a flat greased surface (marble is good) and pull into a thin sheet.

√ *Peanut Butter Ice Cream*

1½ cups milk
 1 cup granulated sugar
 3 tablespoons flour
 ¼ teaspoon salt
 2 eggs, beaten

¾ cup peanut butter
 2 teaspoons vanilla
   extract
 3 cups light cream

1. In a saucepan, combine milk, sugar, flour, and salt. Cook, stirring, on medium heat until slightly thickened (approximately 15 minutes).
2. Stir a few tablespoons of the hot milk mixture into the beaten eggs. Return milk-egg mixture to saucepan and

cook, stirring constantly, for 2 minutes. Remove from heat.

3. Combine and blend well 1 cup of the hot milk mixture with the peanut butter. Then stir peanut butter into milk mixture. Cool.

4. Add vanilla and light cream to milk mixture.

5. Churn-freeze.

Makes ½ gallon

Peanut Butter and Maple Ice Cream

1 cup peanut butter
1½ cups maple syrup

⅛ teaspoon salt
4½ cups heavy cream

1. Mix together peanut butter, maple syrup, salt, and heavy cream.

2. Churn-freeze.

Makes ½ gallon

Peanut Orange Ice Cream

4 tablespoons grated orange rind
½ cup water
1½ cups granulated sugar
¼ teaspoon salt
3 eggs
1 tablespoon unflavored gelatin

2 cups fresh orange juice
2 cups heavy cream, lightly whipped
¾ cup coarsely chopped peanuts
2 teaspoons fresh lemon juice

1. In top of double boiler, combine orange rind and water. Boil for 2 minutes.

2. Add sugar and salt to hot orange rind. Mix together and then strain through a sieve.

3. While beating eggs vigorously, slowly add hot strained orange syrup to the eggs. Return combined mixture to the top of double boiler. Cook, stirring, until thickened.

4. Combine gelatin and 3 tablespoons of the orange juice. Let stand 5 minutes and then add to the hot mixture. Cool.

5. Add remaining orange juice, lightly whipped heavy cream, chopped peanuts, and lemon juice to the cooled mixture.

6. Churn-freeze.

Makes ½ gallon

Pecan Date Ice Cream

1½ cups pitted dates
⅓ cup brandy
1½ cups sweetened
    condensed milk
1 cup water
½ teaspoon salt
1 tablespoon vanilla
    extract

1 tablespoon fresh
    lemon juice
½ teaspoon instant
    coffee
2 cups heavy cream
1 cup chopped pecans

1. Chop dates into fine pieces and soak in brandy for 1 hour.

2. Stir together condensed milk, water, salt, vanilla, and lemon juice. Chill in refrigerator for ¾ hour.

3. Add coffee to the heavy cream and whip until stiff.

4. Combine soaked dates, chilled condensed milk mixture, coffee–whipped cream mixture, and pecans.

5. Churn-freeze.

Makes ½ gallon

Persimmon Ice Cream

6 ripe Japanese
  persimmons
¾ cup granulated sugar

4 tablespoons lemon
  juice
3½ cups heavy cream

1. Purée peeled and seeded persimmons in an electric blender.
2. Add sugar, lemon juice, and heavy cream to persimmon purée.
3. Churn-freeze.

Makes ½ gallon

The persimmons used in this recipe are called Japanese or oriental persimmons. They are grown commercially in California. The mature persimmons are approximately 3 inches in diameter, reddish orange in color, and very sweet.

Pignolia Ice Cream

2 cups milk
1 vanilla bean (3
  inches), split
1½ tablespoons flour
¼ teaspoon salt

1 cup granulated sugar
2 egg yolks
2 egg whites
2 cups heavy cream
½ cup pignolia nuts

1. In a saucepan, combine milk and split vanilla bean. Heat to a boil.
2. Add flour and salt to hot milk. Cook, stirring, on medium heat until slightly thickened.
3. Stir sugar into the hot thickened mixture.
4. Beat egg yolks, adding small amount of the hot milk mixture while beating. Then add beaten egg yolks to hot milk. Cook, stirring, for 1 minute. Strain.
5. Beat egg whites until stiff.

6. Fold egg whites into hot mixture. Cool.
7. Add cream and pignolia nuts to cooled mixture.
8. Churn-freeze.

Makes ½ gallon

Pineapple Ice Cream I

3 cups grated fresh   1½ cups granulated sugar
    pineapple   3 cups heavy cream

1. Purée grated pineapple in an electric blender. Combine pineapple with sugar. Let stand for 3 hours in the refrigerator.
2. Lightly whip cream and fold into pineapple.
3. Churn-freeze.

Makes ½ gallon

Pineapple Ice Cream II

1 cup sour cream
2 cups sweetened
   condensed milk

2 cups milk
2 cups canned crushed
   pineapple, drained

1. Stir together sour cream, condensed milk, regular milk, and crushed pineapple.
2. Churn-freeze.

Makes ½ gallon

Pineapple, Coconut, and Honey Ice Cream

¾ cup honey
2 eggs
1½ cups heavy cream
1½ cups light cream
1 teaspoon vanilla
   extract
¼ teaspoon lemon
   extract

⅛ teaspoon salt
½ cup canned flaked
   coconut
1½ cups canned crushed
   pineapple, drained

1. Mix together honey and eggs. Beat with rotary beater until well blended.
2. Add heavy cream, light cream, vanilla and lemon extracts, salt, coconut, and pineapple to the egg-honey mixture.
3. Churn-freeze.

Makes ½ gallon

Pineapple Marshmallow Ice Cream

2 cups evaporated milk
30 marshmallows
⅛ teaspoon salt
⅔ cup fresh orange juice

1 cup canned crushed
pineapple, drained
2 cups heavy cream,
whipped

1. In top of double boiler, combine evaporated milk and marshmallows. Heat, stirring, until marshmallows melt and mixture is blended. Cool.
2. Add salt, orange juice, crushed pineapple, and whipped heavy cream.
3. Churn-freeze.

Makes ½ gallon

Pineapple Nut Ice Cream

1½ cups canned crushed
pineapple, undrained
2 teaspoons unflavored
gelatin
¾ cup granulated sugar
2½ cups sour cream

½ teaspoon vanilla
extract
¾ cup pecans, chopped
2 cups heavy cream,
stiffly whipped

1. Drain the pineapple juice from the crushed pineapple. Reserve juice.
2. Dissolve gelatin in one tablespoon pineapple juice.
3. In saucepan, add sugar to remaining pineapple juice. Bring to a boil. Cool slightly.
4. Add dissolved gelatin, pineapple, sour cream, vanilla, and pecans to slightly cooled mixture. Mix well. Chill in refrigerator for one hour.

5. Fold stiffly whipped heavy cream into chilled mixture.
6. Still-freeze.

Makes ½ gallon

Pink Peppermint Ice Cream

2 cups evaporated milk
1 pound peppermint candy

2 cups heavy cream
¼ teaspoon salt

1. Pour undiluted evaporated milk over the peppermint candy. Let stand 6 to 8 hours in the refrigerator.
2. Pour mixture through a cheesecloth to strain out undissolved particles of candy.
3. Whip heavy cream with salt until stiff and fold into peppermint mixture.
4. Churn-freeze.

Makes ½ gallon

For a shorter preparation time, or if an even mintier flavor is desired, candy may be crushed in a blender or by hand before soaking in the evaporated milk. If the candy is precrushed, the mixture need only stand 2 hours.

√ Pistachio Ice Cream I

6 ounces pistachio nuts
⅛ teaspoon rose water
2¾ cups light cream
1 teaspoon vanilla extract
½ teaspoon almond extract

¼ teaspoon green food coloring
1 cup granulated sugar
⅛ teaspoon salt
2½ cups heavy cream, lightly whipped

1. Shell and blanch pistachio nuts. (To blanch nuts, place nuts in a strainer and pour boiling water over them, followed by a rinse of cold water; then remove nut skins.)

2. Using a mortar and pestle, grind nuts, adding the rose water to the nuts.

3. Add 1¼ cups of the light cream, the vanilla and almond extracts, and food coloring to the nuts.

4. In a saucepan, combine remaining light cream, the sugar, and salt. Cook, stirring constantly, until sugar dissolves. Cool.

5. Combine nut mixture, cooled sugar-cream mixture, and lightly whipped heavy cream.

6. Churn-freeze.

Makes ½ gallon

Pistachio Ice Cream II

½ cup granulated sugar
¼ cup water
⅛ teaspoon salt
¼ teaspoon cream of tartar
4 egg yolks
1 cup ground pistachio nuts

1 teaspoon almond extract
¼ teaspoon green food coloring
4 cups heavy cream

1. In a saucepan, combine sugar, water, salt, and cream of tartar. Boil for 5 minutes.

2. While beating egg yolks vigorously, slowly pour sugar syrup into them.

3. Add nuts, almond extract, food coloring, and cream to the sugar-egg mixture.

4. Churn-freeze.

Makes ½ gallon

Pistachio Marshmallow Ice Cream

2 cups light cream
30 marshmallows
¼ teaspoon green food
coloring
⅛ teaspoon salt
½ teaspoon almond
extract

½ teaspoon vanilla
extract
2 cups heavy cream,
whipped
1 cup ground pistachio
nuts

1. In top of double boiler, combine light cream and marshmallows. Heat, stirring, until marshmallows melt and mixture is blended. Cool for 20 minutes.
2. Add food coloring, salt, almond and vanilla extracts, whipped heavy cream, and pistachio nuts. Mix well.
3. Still-freeze.

Makes ½ gallon

Praline Ice Cream

1 tablespoon butter
1½ cups dark brown
sugar, firmly packed
1 cup pecans, finely
chopped
5 cups light cream

¼ teaspoon salt
1 teaspoon vanilla
extract
¼ teaspoon almond
extract

1. Prepare praline by spreading butter on a baking sheet in an 8-inch square. Press the brown sugar into the butter about ¼ inch thick. Sprinkle with the chopped pecans. Broil until the sugar bubbles. Cool on sheet. Remove and crush into fine pieces.

2. Mix together cream, salt, vanilla and almond extracts, and crushed praline.

3. Churn-freeze.

Makes ½ gallon

Be very careful not to let the sugar burn.

Prune Ice Cream

2 cups prunes
2 cups granulated sugar
¼ teaspoon salt

¼ cup fresh lemon juice
3 cups heavy cream

1. In a saucepan, soak prunes in 4 cups hot water for ½ hour. Then cook the prunes in this water on medium heat until prunes are soft. Drain. Remove the stones and purée prunes in an electric blender.

2. Mix together prune purée, sugar, salt, lemon juice, and heavy cream.

3. Churn-freeze.

Makes ½ gallon

Pumpkin Ice Cream

1 cup cooked fresh
   pumpkin (about 1
   small pumpkin, or
   1 pound)
6 egg yolks
1 cup granulated sugar
¼ teaspoon salt

½ teaspoon ground
   cinnamon
½ teaspoon ground
   nutmeg
½ teaspoon ground
   ginger
4 cups heavy cream

1. Peel, seed, and cut pumpkin into small pieces. Cook pumpkin pieces in boiling water for 30 minutes, until tender. Drain. Purée cooked pumpkin by forcing through a food mill.

2. Beat egg yolks until thick and creamy.

3. In a double boiler, combine pumpkin purée, beaten egg yolks, sugar, salt, cinnamon, nutmeg, and ginger. Cook, stirring, until well blended and thickened. Cool.

4. Lightly whip heavy cream and add cream to the cooled mixture.

5. Churn-freeze.

Makes ½ gallon

Pumpkin Praline Ice Cream

1 tablespoon butter
2 cups dark brown
  sugar, firmly packed
3 eggs
¼ teaspoon salt
1 cup water
1 cup canned pumpkin

1 teaspoon ground
  ginger
1 teaspoon ground
  cinnamon
½ teaspoon ground
  cloves
2½ cups heavy cream

1. Prepare praline by spreading butter on a baking sheet in an 8-inch square. Press 1 cup of the brown sugar into the butter in a layer about ¼ inch thick. Broil until the sugar bubbles (be careful—sugar burns easily). Cool on sheet. Remove and crush into fine pieces.
2. Beat eggs with salt, until fluffy, in electric mixer on high speed.
3. In a saucepan, bring to a boil 1 cup water with remaining cup brown sugar. Boil 5 minutes without stirring.
4. Slowly pour hot sugar syrup into eggs while beating eggs in electric mixer on high speed. Continue beating until cool.
5. Add pumpkin, ginger, cinnamon, cloves, and praline to beaten sugar-egg mixture. Mix well.
6. Lightly whip cream and fold into the mixture.
7. Churn-freeze.

Makes ½ gallon

Quince Ice Cream

2 cups quince pulp and
  juice (about 6
  quinces)
2 cups milk

2 egg yolks, beaten
1 tablespoon flour
1½ cups granulated sugar
⅛ teaspoon salt

1 tablespoon vanilla   2 cups evaporated milk
   extract

1. Peel and quarter fresh quinces. In a covered saucepan, place quinces with water to cover and cook until tender. Drain. Purée cooked quinces by forcing through a food mill.
2. Heat milk to a boil.
3. In top of double boiler, combine beaten egg yolks, flour, sugar, and salt.
4. While beating egg mixture vigorously, slowly add hot milk to the mixture. Cook for 15 minutes, stirring occasionally. Cool.
5. Add vanilla, evaporated milk, and quince pulp and juice to the cooled mixture.
6. Churn-freeze.

Makes ½ gallon

Raisin Ice Cream

1¾ cups raisins   1 cup granulated sugar
2 cups water   ⅛ teaspoon salt
¼ cup fresh lemon juice   1 tablespoon vanilla
1 cup milk   extract
2 cups heavy cream

1. In a saucepan, combine raisins, water, and lemon juice. Let the mixture stand at room temperature until raisins swell. Then cook on low heat, stirring occasionally, for ½ hour. Cool.
2. Add milk, heavy cream, sugar, salt, and vanilla to the cooled raisin mixture.
3. Churn-freeze.

Makes ½ gallon

Raisin Pineapple Ice Cream

⅓ cup maraschino
   cherries, drained
½ cup raisins
⅔ cup canned crushed
   pineapple, drained
1 teaspoon grated
   orange rind
⅓ cup sweet white wine
2 eggs

1¼ cups granulated sugar
2 cups milk
¼ teaspoon salt
1½ cups heavy cream
1¼ teaspoons vanilla
   extract
½ cup pecans, finely
   chopped

1. Mix together cherries, raisins, pineapple, orange rind, and wine. Let mixture soak in refrigerator overnight.
2. Beat together eggs and ½ cup of the sugar.
3. Caramelize remaining ¾ cup sugar. (To caramelize sugar, put sugar in a heavy skillet and cook, stirring constantly, over medium heat—338° F—until sugar turns to a golden brown syrup.)
4. In a saucepan, heat milk to a boil.
5. While beating egg-sugar mixture, pour some of the hot milk into the eggs. Then return egg mixture to the remaining hot milk in the saucepan. Cook, stirring, on low heat until thickened. Cool.
6. Add wine-soaked fruits, caramelized sugar, heavy cream, vanilla, and pecans to the cooled mixture.
7. Churn-freeze.

Makes ½ gallon

Raspberry Marble Ice Cream

3 eggs
1¾ cups light corn syrup
1½ cups milk

2 teaspoons vanilla
   extract
1½ cups heavy cream

3 cups frozen
    raspberries, thawed
    and drained

1. Combine and mix well eggs, 1 cup of the corn syrup, the milk, and vanilla extract.

2. Whip cream and fold into egg mixture.

3. Still-freeze to mush.

4. In a saucepan, combine raspberries and remaining ¾ cup corn syrup. Cook on low heat for 10 minutes. Cool.

5. Beat partially frozen ice cream, until smooth, with a rotary or electric beater.

6. Return ice cream to freezing tray and drop spoonfuls of cooled raspberry syrup into the mixture. Swirl syrup through the ice cream.

7. Still-freeze.

Makes ½ gallon

Raspberry Sour Cream Ice Cream

3 cups fresh raspberries,   1 teaspoon grated lemon
    cleaned and crushed   rind
¾ cup water   ¼ teaspoon salt
¾ cup granulated sugar   3 cups sour cream

1. In a saucepan, combine cleaned crushed raspberries, water, and sugar. Cook on medium heat, stirring, for 5 minutes. Strain through a fine sieve. Cool.

2. Add grated lemon rind, salt, and sour cream to the cooled mixture.

3. Churn-freeze.

Makes ½ gallon

Red Currant and Raspberry Ice Cream

2 pounds fresh red
   currants, cleaned
2 cups fresh raspberries,
   cleaned
1½ cups granulated sugar
¼ cup water

¼ teaspoon salt
½ teaspoon vanilla
   extract
2 cups heavy cream,
   lightly whipped

1. In a bowl, combine cleaned currants and raspberries. Crush the berries against the bowl with a wooden spoon.
2. Mix 1 cup of the sugar with the berries and let the mixture stand for 1 hour. Then cook mixture in a saucepan, on medium heat, stirring, for 15 minutes. Strain.
3. In another saucepan, combine remaining ½ cup sugar and the water. Boil for 5 minutes.
4. Add sugar syrup to hot, strained berry syrup. Cool.
5. Add salt, vanilla, and lightly whipped heavy cream to the cooled mixture.
6. Churn-freeze.

Makes ½ gallon

Red Raspberry Ice Cream

1 quart fresh red
   raspberries
1 cup granulated sugar

⅛ teaspoon salt
3 cups heavy cream,
   lightly whipped

1. Clean and crush the raspberries.
2. Combine raspberries, sugar, and salt. Let stand for 1½ hours in a warm place. Mash and strain.
3. Combine strained raspberry mixture with lightly whipped heavy cream.
4. Churn-freeze.

Makes ½ gallon

Rhubarb Pineapple Ice Cream

2½ cups chopped fresh
    rhubarb
1 cup canned crushed
    pineapple, drained
½ cup granulated sugar

⅛ teaspoon ground
    nutmeg
⅛ teaspoon salt
3 cups evaporated milk

1. In a baking dish, combine rhubarb, crushed pineapple, sugar, nutmeg, and salt. Cover and bake in moderate oven for approximately one hour.
2. Purée baked mixture in an electric blender. Cool.
3. Add evaporated milk to the purée.
4. Churn-freeze.

Makes ½ gallon

Rhubarb Strawberry Ice Cream

2 packages frozen
    rhubarb (10-ounce
    size), thawed and
    undrained
⅛ teaspoon salt
1⅓ cups granulated sugar

2 packages frozen
    strawberries (10-ounce
    size), thawed and
    drained
3 cups heavy cream,
    lightly whipped

1. In a baking dish, bake thawed rhubarb, salt, and sugar in 300° F oven for 45 minutes. Stir every 15 minutes while baking. Cool.
2. Purée cooled mixture and thawed strawberries in an electric blender.
3. Add lightly whipped cream to the purée.
4. Churn-freeze.

Makes ½ gallon

Rice Almond Ice Cream

¾ cup rice
½ cup blanched almonds
4 cups light cream
1 cup granulated sugar

3 egg yolks, beaten
1 tablespoon orange
flower water (see
page 46)

1. In a saucepan, combine rice, almonds, and 2 cups of the light cream. Cook until rice is tender.
2. In an electric blender, blend hot rice-almond mixture until it is smooth.
3. Return blended mixture to saucepan and add sugar and beaten egg yolks. Cook on medium heat, stirring constantly, for 5 minutes. Cool.
4. Add remaining 2 cups light cream and the orange flower water to the cooled mixture.
5. Churn-freeze.

Makes ½ gallon

Roquefort Ice Cream

1 pound Roquefort
cheese, grated
2 cups milk

4½ cups heavy cream,
whipped

1. In top of double boiler, combine grated cheese and the milk. Cook, stirring, until cheese melts and blends with milk. Cool.
2. Add whipped heavy cream to the cooled cheese mixture. Mix well.
3. Still-freeze.

Makes ½ gallon

Rose Ice Cream

6½ cups heavy cream
 2 teaspoons rose water
⅛ teaspoon salt

¾ cup granulated sugar
¼ teaspoon red food
    coloring

1. Combine heavy cream, rose water, salt, sugar, and food coloring.
2. Churn-freeze.

Makes ½ gallon

Shredded Coconut Ice Cream

1 cup canned shredded
   coconut
1¼ cups sweetened
    condensed milk
3 cups heavy cream,
   lightly whipped

1½ teaspoons vanilla
    extract
⅛ teaspoon salt
2 cups milk

1. Mix together coconut, condensed milk, lightly whipped cream, vanilla, salt, and milk.
2. Churn-freeze.

Makes ½ gallon

Snow Ice Cream

½ cup heavy cream
¼ cup granulated sugar
½ teaspoon vanilla
   extract

1 2-quart bowl of clean,
   freshly fallen snow

1. Stir together cream, sugar, and vanilla.
2. Lightly stirring, pour cream mixture over snow.
3. Serve immediately!

Makes ½ gallon

Snowman makers adore snow-eating. Perhaps because this treat combines the child's rich imaginative world of pretend with the world of actuality; snow ice cream makes toddlers' eyes twinkle with excitement. I have found that the suggestion "Come in, bring some snow and we'll make ice cream" works wonders if a child's toes need warming and he is reluctant to come into the house.

Spearmint Raisin Ice Cream

1   cup raisins
¾   cup granulated sugar
2   cups milk
1   egg yolk
¼   teaspoon salt
1   teaspoon vanilla
    extract

1   teaspoon spearmint
    extract
⅛   teaspoon green food
    coloring
3   cups heavy cream

1. Steam raisins. (To steam raisins, place colander holding raisins into a covered pan with boiling water in the bottom of the pan. Be certain that the raisins are above the water level and that the lid fits tightly so the steam will not escape. Let raisins steam for 15 minutes.) Cool.

2. Caramelize ½ cup of the sugar. (To caramelize sugar, put sugar in a heavy skillet and cook, stirring constantly, over medium heat—338° F—until sugar turns to a golden brown syrup.)

3. In top of double boiler, heat 1 cup of the milk to boil.

4. Beat egg yolk, and while beating add a little hot milk. Then return egg mixture to top of double boiler.

5. Add caramelized sugar and remaining ¼ cup granulated sugar to the egg yolk–milk mixture. Cook, stirring, until slightly thickened. Cool.

6. Add remaining 1 cup milk, salt, vanilla, spearmint, food coloring, heavy cream, and raisins to the cooled mixture.

7. Churn-freeze.

Makes ½ gallon

If fresh spearmint is used, chop about 4 sprigs and combine with milk in top of double boiler. Then strain the mixture.

Spiced Peach Ice Cream

1   jar spiced peaches
    (30-ounce size),
    crushed
2   eggs, beaten
½   cup granulated sugar
1   cup milk
2   tablespoons fresh
    lemon juice

¼   teaspoon salt
½   teaspoon almond
    extract
⅓   cup brandy
2   cups heavy cream,
    lightly whipped

1. Pour peach syrup into a saucepan, straining out whole spices.

2. Add eggs, sugar, milk, lemon juice, and salt to the syrup. Cook on medium heat until mixture thickens. Cool.

3. Add almond extract, brandy, lightly whipped heavy cream, and crushed peaches to the cooled mixture.

4. Churn-freeze.

Makes ½ gallon

Spumoni

1½ cups water
1¼ cups granulated sugar
2   vanilla beans (1-inch
    size)
10 egg yolks
5   egg whites
¼   teaspoon salt
3   cups heavy cream,
    whipped
2   teaspoons candied
    angelica

2   teaspoons citron
2   teaspoons candied
    apricot
2   teaspoons candied
    lemon
2   teaspoons candied
    orange peel
4   tablespoons blanched
    almonds

1. In a saucepan, combine water, sugar, and vanilla beans. Boil for 5 minutes. Remove vanilla beans.

2. Beat egg yolks until thick and creamy. While beating

egg yolks, gradually beat in the hot sugar syrup until syrup and eggs are well combined.

3. Beat egg whites until stiff, combine with salt and whipped heavy cream, and add to the egg yolk mixture.
4. Add candied fruits and almonds to the mixture.
5. Still-freeze.

Makes ½ gallon

Strawberry Ice Cream I

2 cups heavy cream
4 egg yolks
1 piece lemon peel

½ cup granulated sugar
1 quart fresh
   strawberries

1. In a saucepan, mix together cream, egg yolks, and lemon pecl. Cook on low heat, stirring, until thickened.
2. Add sugar to the mixture. Strain and cool.
3. Purée strawberries and add to the cooled mixture.
4. Churn-freeze.

Makes ½ gallon

Strawberry Ice Cream II

2 packages frozen
   strawberries (10-ounce
   size), thawed and
   drained
1½ tablespoons fresh
   lemon juice
2 tablespoons lemon
   peel

½ teaspoon ground
   allspice
1½ cups condensed milk
3 cups heavy cream,
   whipped

1. In an electric blender, mix together strawberries, lemon juice, lemon peel, and allspice. Blend for 30 seconds on high speed.
2. Add condensed milk and whipped heavy cream to the blended mixture. Mix well.
3. Still-freeze.

Makes ½ gallon

Strawberry Ice Cream III

2¾ cups fresh strawberries
2 cups granulated sugar

2¾ cups heavy cream,
  lightly whipped

1. Press strawberries through a sieve or purée in an electric blender.
2. Add sugar and lightly whipped heavy cream to strawberry pulp.
3. Churn-freeze.

Makes ½ gallon

Strawberry Kirsch Ice Cream

2½ cups frozen
  strawberries, thawed
  and drained
1½ cups water
¾ cup granulated sugar

Juice of 1 lemon
3 cups heavy cream,
  lightly whipped
¼ cup kirsch

1. Purée thawed frozen strawberries.
2. In a saucepan, combine water and sugar. Boil for 5 minutes. Cool.
3. Combine strawberry purée, sugar syrup, juice of the lemon, lightly whipped cream, and kirsch.
4. Churn-freeze.

Makes ½ gallon

Strawberry Sour Cream Ice Cream

2 packages frozen
  strawberries (10-ounce
  size), thawed and
  drained

2 cups granulated sugar
4 cups sour cream

1. Mix together thawed strawberries, sugar, and sour cream.
2. Churn-freeze.

Makes ½ gallon

√ Swiss Chocolate and Almond Ice Cream

3 cups light cream	½ cup granulated sugar
2 eggs	½ teaspoon vanilla
1½ teaspoons flour	extract
8 ounces Swiss dark chocolate	2 cups heavy cream, lightly whipped
¼ teaspoon salt	1 cup whole almonds

1. In top of double boiler, heat 2 cups of the light cream.
2. Beat together eggs, flour, and remaining cup light cream and, while stirring vigorously, add to heated cream.
3. Cook, stirring, until slightly thickened. Then add Swiss chocolate, salt, and sugar. Continue cooking and stirring mixture until chocolate is melted. Cool.
4. Add vanilla, lightly whipped heavy cream, and almonds.
5. Churn-freeze.

Makes ½ gallon

Tangerine Ice Cream

⅔ cup granulated sugar	3 tablespoons mandarin liqueur
1½ cups fresh tangerine juice	2½ cups heavy cream, whipped
2 cups grated fresh coconut	
½ cup chopped tangerine pulp (approximately 10 tangerines)	

1. In a saucepan, combine sugar and tangerine juice. Boil for 5 minutes. Cool.
2. Add coconut, tangerine pulp, mandarin liqueur, and whipped heavy cream to cooled sugar-tangerine syrup. Mix well.
3. Still-freeze to mush.
4. Beat.
5. Still-freeze until firm.

Makes ½ gallon

Tea Ice Cream

3 cups milk	¼ teaspoon salt
4½ tablespoons tea	3 cups heavy cream
2 cups granulated sugar	1 teaspoon finely grated
4 egg yolks, beaten	orange rind

1. In a saucepan, heat milk to a boil. Remove from heat.
2. Add tea to heated milk. Cover and let stand for 6 minutes.
3. Add sugar to tea-milk mixture.
4. Strain mixture into the top of a double boiler.
5. Add beaten egg yolks and salt to the tea-milk mixture. Cook, stirring constantly, until thickened. Strain and cool.
6. Add heavy cream and orange rind to the custard.
7. Churn-freeze.

Makes ½ gallon

Toasted Coconut Ice Cream

1½ cups canned coconut, toasted and crumbled	¼ teaspoon salt
	3 cups milk
4 tablespoons quick-cooking tapioca	½ cup light corn syrup
	¾ cup granulated sugar

3 egg whites
2 cups heavy cream,
   lightly whipped

1 tablespoon vanilla
   extract

1. To toast coconut, spread it in a flat pan. Stirring frequently, bake in a 350° F oven for 12 minutes, until lightly browned.

2. In top of double boiler, combine tapioca, salt, and milk. Cook, stirring occasionally, for approximately 15 minutes or until mixture is thickened.

3. Add the corn syrup and sugar and continue to cook until sugar is dissolved. Cool.

4. Beat egg whites until stiff.

5. Fold egg whites, lightly whipped cream, vanilla, and coconut into the cooled tapioca mixture.

6. Churn-freeze.

Makes ½ gallon

Tutti-Frutti Ice Cream

1 cup granulated sugar
¾ cup canned crushed
   pineapple, drained
3 bananas, peeled and
   mashed
¼ cup maraschino
   cherries, drained
4 fresh oranges, peeled,
   seeded, and cut into
   small pieces

2 tablespoons fresh
   lemon juice
2 tablespoons
   unflavored gelatin
¼ cup cold water
½ cup chopped almonds
3 cups heavy cream,
   lightly whipped

1. Combine sugar, pineapple, bananas, cherries, oranges, and lemon juice. Mix well.

2. Soften gelatin in water for 5 minutes. Then heat gelatin and water until dissolved.

3. Add dissolved gelatin, almonds, and lightly whipped cream to the fruit mixture.
4. Churn-freeze.

Makes ½ gallon

√ Vanilla Ice Cream I

1 cup granulated sugar
5 cups light cream
¼ teaspoon vanilla
    extract

⅛ teaspoon salt

1. Combine sugar, cream, vanilla, and salt.
2. Churn-freeze.

Makes ½ gallon

√ Vanilla Ice Cream II

5 cups heavy cream
4 egg whites
4 egg yolks

1 cup granulated sugar
1 teaspoon vanilla
    extract

1. Whip heavy cream.
2. Beat egg whites until stiff.
3. Beat egg yolks.
4. Add sugar and vanilla to the whipped cream.
5. Fold together the cream mixture, egg whites, and egg yolks.
6. Still-freeze.

Makes ½ gallon

Vanilla Ice Cream III

2 eggs, beaten
1¼ cups granulated sugar
3 cups milk
2 cups light cream

1 tablespoon vanilla
   extract
¼ teaspoon salt

1. Combine eggs and sugar. Beat with rotary beater until mixture is slightly thickened.
2. Add, mixing well, the milk, light cream, vanilla, and salt to the egg mixture.
3. Churn-freeze.

Makes ½ gallon

Vanilla Ice Cream IV

1 tablespoon unflavored
   gelatin
½ cup water
6 cups heavy cream

1½ cups granulated sugar
1 cup evaporated milk
1 tablespoon vanilla
   extract

1. Combine gelatin and water. Let stand 5 minutes.
2. In a saucepan, heat 2 cups of the heavy cream to a boil. Remove from heat.
3. Add gelatin and sugar to the hot cream. Mix well.
4. Add remaining cream, the evaporated milk, and vanilla to the gelatin mixture.
5. Churn-freeze.

Makes ½ gallon

Vanilla Bean Ice Cream

1 cup granulated sugar	6 egg yolks
½ cup water	1 vanilla bean (3 inches)
⅛ teaspoon salt	6 cups heavy cream
¼ teaspoon cream of tartar	

1. In a saucepan, mix together sugar, water, salt, and cream of tartar. Cook for approximately 10 minutes (until syrup spins a thread).
2. Beat egg yolks until thick, gradually adding sugar syrup to the egg yolks while beating.
3. Remove pulp from the vanilla bean and add pulp and heavy cream to the sugar-egg mixture.
4. Churn-freeze.

Makes ½ gallon

Vanilla Blender Ice Cream

1 cup granulated sugar	1 tablespoon vanilla
1 tablespoon cornstarch	2 cups light cream
⅛ teaspoon salt	4 cups heavy cream
4 egg yolks	

1. In electric blender, combine sugar, cornstarch, salt, egg yolks, vanilla, and light cream. Blend until smooth.
2. Stir in the heavy cream.
3. Churn-freeze.

Makes ½ gallon

Vanilla Pudding Ice Cream

4 cups milk
1 cup light corn syrup
1 box vanilla pudding
  mix (3-ounce size)
1 teaspoon vanilla
  extract

½ teaspoon almond
  extract
1 cup heavy cream,
  lightly whipped

1. In a saucepan, add milk and then corn syrup to pudding mix. Cook, stirring, until slightly thickened. Cool.

2. Add vanilla and almond extracts and lightly whipped cream to pudding mixture.

3. Churn-freeze.

Makes ½ gallon

Vermont Ice Cream

1¾ cups maple syrup
2 eggs, beaten
⅛ teaspoon salt

2 cups milk
3 cups heavy cream,
  lightly whipped

1. In a saucepan, heat maple syrup to a boil.

2. While beating vigorously, slowly pour a few tablespoons hot syrup into eggs and then add all of the eggs to the syrup.

3. Add salt, milk, and lightly whipped cream to the syrup mixture.

4. Churn-freeze.

Makes ½ gallon

White Grape Ice Cream

3 pounds fresh white grapes

1¼ cups granulated sugar

2 cups heavy cream, lightly whipped

1 teaspoon fresh lime juice

⅛ teaspoon ground ginger

1. Heat grapes over low flame, stirring and pressing grapes with a spoon to separate skins and seeds from the pulp.
2. Add sugar to the grapes and continue to cook on low heat for 10 minutes, stirring occasionally.
3. Strain grape juice through a fine sieve. Cool.
4. Add lightly whipped heavy cream, lime juice, and ginger to grape mixture.
5. Churn-freeze.

Makes ½ gallon

This is an ice cream surprise for guests who enjoy unusual treats. There are no color clues. I have some friends with a special knack of discerning individual ingredients in a blend. This one is good and tricky!

X

Milk Sherbet

Banana Milk Sherbet

2½ cups peeled, puréed
    bananas
½ cup granulated sugar
4 cups milk

3 tablespoons fresh
    lemon juice
⅛ teaspoon salt

1. Combine banana purée, sugar, milk, lemon juice, and salt.
2. Churn-freeze.

Makes ½ gallon

Banana Kirsch Milk Sherbet

3 cups peeled, puréed
    bananas
¼ cup plus 2 tablespoons
    kirsch
¾ cup granulated sugar

½ cup light corn syrup
⅛ teaspoon salt
2 egg whites, stiffly
    beaten
3 cups milk

1. In an electric blender, purée bananas, adding kirsch, sugar, corn syrup, and salt while blending.
2. Stir stiffly beaten egg whites and the milk into banana mixture.
3. Still-freeze to mush.
4. Beat.
5. Still-freeze until firm.

Makes ½ gallon

Blackberry Milk Sherbet

1½ cups granulated sugar
1 cup water
⅛ teaspoon salt
2¼ cups strained fresh
    blackberry purée
    (slightly less than 1
    quart blackberries)

3 cups evaporated milk

1. In a saucepan, combine sugar and water. Boil for 5 minutes. Cool.
2. Add salt, blackberry purée, and evaporated milk to the cooled sugar syrup. (To purée blackberries, use an electric blender on medium speed.)
3. Churn-freeze.

Makes ½ gallon

Black Raspberry Milk Sherbet

2 cups granulated sugar
¾ cup water
⅛ teaspoon salt

2 cups canned black
   raspberries, drained
4 cups milk

1. In a saucepan, combine sugar, water, and salt. Boil for 5 minutes. Cool.

2. In an electric blender, purée the black raspberries.
3. Mix together sugar syrup, berry purée, and milk.
4. Churn-freeze.

Makes ½ gallon

Cherry Milk Sherbet

1   quart fresh red   ½   teaspoon almond
    cherries   extract
1¼ cups granulated sugar   4   cups milk

1. Clean and pit cherries and then strain through a colander, reserving juice and pulp.
2. Mix together the cherry juice and pulp with the sugar. Let stand for 1 hour in the refrigerator.
3. Add almond extract and milk to the cherry mixture.
4. Churn-freeze.

Makes ½ gallon

Coffee Milk Sherbet

2   tablespoons   4   cups milk
    unflavored gelatin   ⅛   teaspoon salt
3½ cups water   ½   teaspoon vanilla
¼   cup instant coffee   extract
½   cup granulated sugar

1. Combine gelatin and ¼ cup cold water.
2. In a saucepan, bring remaining water to a boil.
3. Add boiling water to instant coffee.
4. Add softened gelatin and sugar to hot coffee. Cool.
5. Add milk, salt, and vanilla to cooled mixture.
6. Churn-freeze.

Makes ½ gallon

Coffee Cognac Milk Sherbet

1½ cups water
1½ cups granulated sugar
 4 cups milk

½ cup ground coffee
2 tablespoons cognac

1. In a saucepan, combine water and sugar. Bring to a boil and then allow mixture to simmer for 5 minutes. Cool.
2. Heat milk to a boil and then pour hot milk onto ground coffee. Let stand for 20 minutes. Strain through cheesecloth. Cool.
3. Combine cooled sugar syrup, strained coffee-milk, and cognac.
4. Churn-freeze.

Makes ½ gallon

Cranberry Milk Sherbet

4 cups canned cranberry
    sauce
3 tablespoons fresh
    lemon juice

¾ cup fresh orange juice
⅛ teaspoon salt
3 cups milk
6 egg whites

1. Mix together cranberry sauce, lemon juice, orange juice, salt, and milk.
2. Beat egg whites until stiff and stir into the cranberry mixture.
3. Churn-freeze.

Makes ½ gallon

Fruit Cocktail Milk Sherbet

1 pound marshmallows
1½ cups canned
   unsweetened
   pineapple juice
1½ cups canned fruit
   cocktail, drained

½ cup canned pitted
   black cherries,
   drained
2½ cups milk

1. In a saucepan, combine marshmallows and pineapple juice. Heat until marshmallows melt. Cool slightly.
2. Add fruit cocktail, cherries, and milk to the marshmallow mixture.
3. Churn-freeze.

Makes ½ gallon

Grape Milk Sherbet

2½ cups canned or fresh
   grape juice
¾ cup granulated sugar

⅛ teaspoon salt
4 cups milk

1. In a saucepan, combine grape juice, sugar, and salt. Heat, stirring, to a boil. Cool.
2. Add milk to the cooled mixture.
3. Churn-freeze.

Makes ½ gallon

Grape Apple Milk Sherbet

2 pounds fresh apples,
   cored, peeled, and
   sliced
2 pounds fresh grapes

1½ cups granulated sugar
⅛ teaspoon salt
1 cup milk

1. In a saucepan, combine apples, grapes, sugar, and salt. Cook, stirring occasionally, on medium heat until apples are soft. Press the mixture through a sieve. Cool.
2. Add milk to the cooled mixture.
3. Churn-freeze.

Makes ½ gallon

Grape Pineapple Milk Sherbet

2 *cups granulated sugar*
2 *cups canned grape juice*
Juice of 2 lemons

1 *cup canned crushed pineapple, drained*
3 *cups milk*

1. Mix together sugar, grape juice, juice of the lemons, the pineapple, and milk.
2. Churn-freeze.

Makes ½ gallon

Guava Milk Sherbet

1 *tablespoon unflavored gelatin*
¼ *cup water*
4 *cups milk*
1¼ *cups honey*

2 *cups canned guavas, drained and puréed*
½ *teaspoon ground ginger*

1. Soften gelatin in water.
2. In a saucepan, combine milk and honey. Heat to a boil. Remove from heat.
3. Add gelatin to hot honey-milk mixture. Mix well. Cool slightly.
4. Add puréed guavas and ginger to slightly cooled mixture.
5. Churn-freeze.

Makes ½ gallon

Honey Fruit Milk Sherbet

1½ cups honey
1 cup canned crushed
   pineapple, undrained
⅛ teaspoon salt
⅔ cup chopped fresh
   orange sections

1 cup chopped peeled
   peaches
3½ cups milk
1 cup light cream
3 tablespoons dry or
   sweet sherry

1. Combine honey, pineapple and juice, and salt. Beat with rotary beater until well mixed.
2. Add orange sections, peaches, milk, light cream, and sherry to the honey mixture.
3. Churn-freeze.

Makes ½ gallon

Jello Milk Sherbet

1 package jello
1 cup boiling water
1½ cups granulated sugar

4 tablespoons fresh
   lemon juice
4 cups milk

1. Dissolve jello in boiling water.
2. Add sugar to hot jello. Cool to lukewarm.
3. Add lemon juice and milk to jello mixture.
4. Churn-freeze.

Makes ½ gallon

Lemon Milk Sherbet

½ cup fresh lemon juice
1 tablespoon finely
   grated lemon rind

1½ cups granulated sugar
5 cups milk
⅛ teaspoon salt

1. Mix together lemon juice, lemon rind, and sugar. Let stand at room temperature for 1½ hours.
2. Add milk and salt to the lemon mixture.
3. Churn-freeze.

Makes ½ gallon

Lemon Orange Milk Sherbet

Juice of 6 lemons
Juice of 2 oranges
3 tablespoons
*   cornstarch*

⅛ teaspoon salt
3 cups water
3 cups condensed milk

1. Strain juice of the lemons and oranges.
2. Add cornstarch and salt to ½ cup water. Mix well.
3. In top of double boiler, combine lemon juice, orange juice, cornstarch mixture, remaining 2½ cups water, and condensed milk. Cook, stirring, until mixture thickens slightly. Cool.
4. Churn-freeze.

Makes ½ gallon

Lime Milk Sherbet

¼ cup green maraschino
*   cherries, drained and*
*   chopped*
1½ cups granulated sugar
½ cup plus 1 tablespoon
*   fresh lime juice*

5 cups milk
Few drops green food
*   coloring*

1. Mix together cherries, sugar, lime juice, milk, and food coloring.
2. Churn-freeze.

Makes ½ gallon

Loganberry Milk Sherbet

1 teaspoon unflavored
  gelatin
1 tablespoon cold water
1 cup fresh loganberry
  juice and pulp
1 teaspoon finely grated
  lemon rind

2 tablespoons fresh
  lemon juice
1 cup granulated sugar
4 cups milk

1. Soften gelatin in the cold water.
2. In a saucepan, mix together loganberry juice and pulp, lemon rind and juice, and sugar. Cook, stirring, on low heat until sugar dissolves.
3. Add softened gelatin to the hot mixture. Cool.
4. Add milk to the cooled mixture.
5. Churn-freeze.

Makes ½ gallon

Orange Milk Sherbet I

2 Junket rennet tablets
2 tablespoons cold
  water
4 cups milk
1¾ cups granulated sugar
⅛ teaspoon salt
1 cup fresh orange juice

⅓ cup fresh lemon juice
2 teaspoons finely
  grated lemon rind
⅛ teaspoon red food
  coloring
⅛ teaspoon yellow food
  coloring

1. Combine rennet tablets and cold water.
2. In a saucepan, combine milk, sugar, and salt. Heat, stirring, until lukewarm. Remove from heat.
3. Add dissolved rennet tablets to the lukewarm milk mixture. Stir briefly and then let stand at room temperature until cool.
4. Add orange and lemon juice, lemon rind, and food coloring to the mixture.
5. Churn-freeze.

Makes ½ gallon

Orange Milk Sherbet II

1½ cups water
 1 cup granulated sugar
 ⅛ teaspoon salt
 2 cups fresh orange juice
    and pulp

2 tablespoons fresh
   lemon juice
2½ cups milk

1. In a saucepan, combine water, sugar, and salt. Boil 10 minutes. Cool.

2. Combine orange juice and pulp, lemon juice, cooled sugar syrup, and milk.

3. Churn-freeze.

Makes ½ gallon

Orange Pekoe Tea Milk Sherbet

2 teaspoons unflavored   1 cup granulated sugar
   gelatin   4 egg yolks
¼ cup water   ⅛ teaspoon salt
2 cups milk   4 cups fresh orange juice
3 tablespoons orange   4 egg whites, stiffly
   pekoe tea   beaten

1. Soften gelatin in the water.
2. In the top of a double boiler, heat milk to a boil.
3. Pour hot milk onto tea leaves. Let stand 5 minutes. Strain, then return mixture to double boiler.
4. While beating vigorously, add softened gelatin, sugar, egg yolks, and salt to hot milk-tea mixture. Cook, stirring, on medium heat until slightly thickened. Cool.
5. Add orange juice and stiffly beaten egg whites to the cooled mixture. Mix well.
6. Churn-freeze.

Makes ½ gallon

Peach Milk Sherbet

3½ cups peach pulp purée   1½ cups granulated sugar
   (about 3½ pounds   ⅛ teaspoon salt
   peaches)   2¼ cups milk

1. Combine peach purée, sugar, salt, and milk. (To purée peaches: peel, pit, and blend them in an electric blender on medium speed.)
2. Churn-freeze.

Makes ½ gallon

Pear Milk Sherbet

1½ pounds ripe Bartlett
    pears, peeled and
    cored
 3 tablespoons fresh
    lemon juice

2 cinnamon sticks
   (3-inch size)
¼ cup granulated sugar
¾ cup water
3 cups light cream

1. In a saucepan, combine pears, lemon juice, cinnamon, sugar, and water. Cook, stirring occasionally, on low heat until pears are tender. Press mixture through a sieve. Cool.
2. Add light cream to the cooled pear mixture.
3. Churn-freeze.

Makes ½ gallon

Pineapple Milk Sherbet

2 cups water
1 cup granulated sugar
2 cups milk

2 cups canned crushed
   pineapple, drained

1. In a saucepan, combine water and sugar. Boil for 5 minutes. Cool.
2. Mix together sugar syrup, milk, and crushed pineapple.
3. Churn-freeze.

Makes ½ gallon

Pineapple Strawberry Milk Sherbet

3 cups fresh
   strawberries, washed
   and hulled
¾ cup fresh pineapple,
   crushed

¾ cup granulated sugar
¾ cup water
2 tablespoons fresh
   lemon juice
2 cups milk

1. Mix together strawberries, pineapple, and sugar. Press against side of bowl with a wooden spoon. Let stand for 1 hour.
2. Add water, lemon juice, and milk to crushed fruit.
3. Churn-freeze.

Makes ½ gallon

Plum Milk Sherbet

2 cups fresh plums,
   cooked
2 egg whites
¾ cup granulated sugar
1 cup light corn syrup

2 cups milk
¼ cup fresh lemon juice
¼ teaspoon red food
   coloring

1. Purée cooked plums. (To purée plums: peel, pit, and blend in an electric blender on medium speed.)
2. Beat egg whites until stiff peaks form.
3. Blend sugar, corn syrup, and milk into the plum purée.
4. Fold egg whites into the plum mixture.
5. Add food coloring.
6. Churn-freeze.

Makes ½ gallon

Prune Milk Sherbet

2 tablespoons
   unflavored gelatin
¼ cup cold water
1 cup boiling water
3 cups canned prune
   juice

1 tablespoon fresh
   lemon juice
⅛ teaspoon salt
3 cups milk

1. Soften gelatin in the ¼ cup cold water. Let stand for 5 minutes.
2. Add 1 cup boiling water to gelatin. Cool slightly.
3. Mix together gelatin, prune juice, lemon juice, salt, and milk.
4. Churn-freeze.

Makes ½ gallon

Quick Fruit Milk Sherbet

2 packages frozen fruit (such as raspberries) (10-ounce size), thawed and undrained	4 cups milk 1 cup granulated sugar ⅛ teaspoon salt

1. Mash frozen fruit with a fork.
2. Mix together fruit, milk, sugar, and salt.
3. Still-freeze to mush.
4. Beat.
5. Still-freeze until firm.

Makes ½ gallon

Raspberry Milk Sherbet

3 packages frozen raspberries (10-ounce size), undrained ¾ cup granulated sugar 3 cups milk	2 tablespoons light corn syrup 3 tablespoons fresh lemon juice

1. Let berries thaw and then purée in an electric blender. Strain through a sieve to remove seeds.
2. In a saucepan, combine sugar, milk, and corn syrup. Cook, stirring, until sugar dissolves.

3. Mix together raspberry purée, sugar-milk syrup, and lemon juice.
4. Churn-freeze.

Makes ½ gallon

Rhubarb Milk Sherbet

1½ cups cooked rhubarb   1½ cups granulated sugar
     purée (about 10   ¼ cup fresh lemon juice
     medium-size stalks, or   ⅛ teaspoon salt
     1½ pounds)   3¾ cups milk
¾ cup light corn syrup

1. Mix together rhubarb purée, corn syrup, sugar, lemon juice, salt, and milk.
2. Churn-freeze.

Makes ½ gallon

Before cooking rhubarb, remove the leaves and ends of the stems. (If the rhubarb is young and tender, it does not need to be peeled.) Cut stalks into short pieces and place in saucepan with water to cover. Cook on medium heat until tender. Drain. To purée the cooked rhubarb, force through a food mill.

Sour Cream Raspberry Sherbet

3 cups fresh ripe   1¼ cups granulated sugar
    raspberries, washed   1 cup water
    and mashed   3 cups sour cream

1. In a saucepan, combine mashed raspberries, sugar, and water. Boil for 5 minutes. Strain through a sieve. Chill for 1 hour.
2. Add sour cream to chilled raspberry mixture. Mix well.

3. Churn-freeze or still-freeze to mush.
4. Beat.
5. Still-freeze until firm.

Makes ½ gallon

Spanish Milk Sherbet

5 cups milk
¾ cup granulated sugar
6 egg yolks, beaten

6 egg whites
¼ teaspoon vanilla
  extract

1. In a saucepan, mix together milk, sugar, and beaten egg yolks. Cook, stirring, until mixture begins to simmer. Cool.
2. Beat egg whites until stiff. Add egg whites and vanilla to cooled custard.
3. Churn-freeze.

Makes ½ gallon

Strawberry Milk Sherbet I

1 quart fresh
  strawberries
1 cup granulated sugar
1¼ cups milk

¼ cup fresh orange juice
⅛ teaspoon ground
  cinnamon

1. Clean and slice strawberries.
2. Combine strawberries and sugar. Let stand for 2 hours. Then purée strawberries in an electric blender. Strain to remove seeds.
3. Add milk, orange juice, and cinnamon to the strawberry purée.
4. Churn-freeze.

Makes ½ gallon

Strawberry Milk Sherbet II

1 tablespoon unflavored gelatin	2 teaspoons fresh lemon juice
1 cup water	4 cups frozen strawberries, drained
1 cup granulated sugar	
1 cup instant dry milk	

1. Soak gelatin in the water until it softens.
2. In a saucepan, combine sugar, dry milk, and softened gelatin. Cook, stirring, until hot but not boiling. Cool.
3. Still-freeze to a mush.
4. Beat, adding lemon juice and strawberries to the frozen mixture.
5. Still-freeze until firm.

Makes ½ gallon

Tangerine Buttermilk Sherbet

2 tablespoons unflavored gelatin	2 cups frozen concentrated tangerine juice
1 cup water	4 cups buttermilk
1¼ cups granulated sugar	

1. Soften gelatin in water for 5 minutes.
2. In top of double boiler, combine gelatin and sugar. Heat, stirring, until gelatin and sugar dissolve.
3. Add tangerine concentrate and buttermilk to the gelatin-sugar mixture.
4. Churn-freeze.

Makes ½ gallon

Tutti-Frutti Milk Sherbet

1 package strawberry jello (3-ounce size)	1 cup hot water
	1 cup granulated sugar

3   bananas, peeled and   1   cup canned
    puréed   unsweetened
1   cup fresh orange juice   pineapple juice
1½ tablespoons fresh   1½ cups light cream
    lemon juice

1. Add strawberry jello to hot water. Stir to dissolve jello and then add sugar.

2. Combine banana purée, orange juice, lemon juice, pineapple juice, and light cream. Mix well.

3. Add fruit-cream mixture to jello.

4. Churn-freeze.

Makes ½ gallon

Watermelon Milk Sherbet

1½ tablespoons   ¼   teaspoon ground
    unflavored gelatin   nutmeg
5   cups watermelon   1½ teaspoons fresh lemon
    purée (about 1   juice
    large watermelon)   1½ cups milk
1½ cups granulated sugar

1. Soften gelatin in ½ cup of the watermelon purée. Let stand 5 minutes at room temperature and then heat gently to dissolve gelatin. Cool slightly.

2. Add remaining watermelon purée, sugar, nutmeg, lemon juice, and milk to the gelatin mixture.

3. Churn-freeze.

Makes ½ gallon

This same recipe is perfect for Cranshaw melon milk sherbet. Five cups Cranshaw melon purée equal about a 5-pound melon. The Cranshaw melon is so flavorful, the resulting milk sherbet is delicious.

XI

Sherbet

Apple Sherbet

12 large apples, peeled,
    cored, and sliced
1⅓ cups granulated sugar
  ¼ teaspoon salt

½ teaspoon ground
  cinnamon
3¼ cups water

   1. In a saucepan, combine apples, sugar, salt, cinnamon, and water. Cook, stirring occasionally, on medium heat until apples are soft. Press the mixture through a sieve. Cool.
   2. Churn-freeze.

Makes ½ gallon

Apple Orange Sherbet

4½ cups fresh or canned apple juice

2½ cups fresh orange juice
¼ cup granulated sugar

1. Mix together apple juice, orange juice, and sugar.
2. Churn-freeze.

Makes ½ gallon

Applesauce Cider Sherbet

1½ tablespoons
    unflavored gelatin
¼ cup cold water
3½ cups applesauce

3 cups cider
¾ cup granulated sugar
1 tablespoon fresh
    lemon juice

1. Soften gelatin in ¼ cup cold water. Let stand for 5 minutes. Then heat gently to dissolve gelatin.
2. Mix together dissolved gelatin, apple sauce, cider, sugar, and lemon juice.
3. Churn-freeze.

Makes ½ gallon

Apricot Sherbet

4 cups water
1 cup granulated sugar
2½ cups canned apricot
    nectar

2 tablespoons fresh
    lemon juice

1. In a saucepan, combine water and sugar. Boil for ! minutes. Cool.
2. Add apricot nectar and lemon juice to sugar syrup.
3. Churn-freeze.

Makes ½ gallon

Apricot Grapefruit Sherbet

1¾ cups granulated sugar
1½ cups water
1½ cups puréed cooked
    apricots (about 9 fresh
    apricots)
2 cups fresh grapefruit
    juice

½ tablespoon fresh
    lemon juice
3 egg whites, stiffly
    beaten

1. In a saucepan, combine sugar and water. Boil for 5 minutes. Cool.
2. Cook apricots and press through sieve or purée in an electric blender. Cool.
3. Combine and mix well cold sugar syrup, grapefruit juice, apricot purée, and lemon juice.
4. Fold in stiffly beaten egg whites.
5. Churn-freeze.

Makes ½ gallon

Apricot Lime Sherbet

3½ cups canned apricot
    nectar
2 cups water

1½ cups granulated sugar
½ cup fresh lime juice

1. Mix together apricot nectar, water, sugar, and lime juice.
2. Churn-freeze.

Makes ½ gallon

Avocado Sherbet

4 cups avocado purée
    (about 5 large
    avocados)
1 teaspoon salt
¼ cup fresh lime juice

4 tablespoons fresh
    lemon juice
1 teaspoon finely grated
    lemon rind
1⅓ cups honey

1. Combine avocado purée, salt, lime juice, lemon juice, lemon rind, and honey. (To purée avocados, use an electric blender on high speed.) Mix well.
2. Still-freeze to mush.
3. Beat.
4. Still-freeze until firm.

Makes ½ gallon

Banana Orange Sherbet

1 cup water	2 tablespoons fresh
1½ cups granulated sugar	lemon juice
6 medium sized bananas,	2 egg whites, stiffly
peeled and mashed	beaten
2½ cups fresh orange juice	

1. In a saucepan, combine water and sugar. Boil for 5 minutes. Cool.
2. Combine and mix well cooled sugar syrup, banana pulp, orange juice, and lemon juice.
3. Churn-freeze to mush.
4. Open freezer and stir stiffly beaten egg whites into mixture.
5. Churn-freeze until firm.

Makes ½ gallon

Blackberry Sherbet

4 cups water	2 tablespoons fresh
1 cup granulated sugar	lemon juice
3 cups fresh blackberry	
purée (about 1 full	
quart blackberries)	

1. In a saucepan, combine water and sugar. Boil for 5 minutes. Cool.
2. Add blackberry purée and lemon juice to sugar syrup. (To purée blackberries, use an electric blender on medium speed.)
3. Churn-freeze.

Makes ½ gallon

Black Currant Leaf Sherbet

3 cups water
2 cups granulated sugar
2 cups black currant
   leaves (young ones)

Juice of 6 lemons

1. In a saucepan, mix together water and sugar. Boil for 5 minutes.
2. Add currant leaves to the sugar syrup. Boil for 3 more minutes. Remove from heat. Let stand for 2½ hours, covered. Strain.
3. Squeeze the lemons, and add the juice to the mixture.
4. Churn-freeze.

Makes ½ gallon

Black Raspberry Sherbet

1 quart fresh black
   raspberries, cleaned
1¼ cups granulated sugar

1½ cups water
¼ cup fresh lemon juice

1. Purée raspberries in a colander or electric blender. Strain through a sieve to remove seeds.
2. In a saucepan, combine sugar and water. Boil for 5 minutes. Cool.
3. Mix together puréed raspberries, sugar syrup, and lemon juice.
4. Churn-freeze.

Makes ½ gallon

Boysenberry Sherbet

1 tablespoon unflavored
  gelatin
¼ cup cold water
6 cups puréed fresh
  boysenberries (about
  2 full quarts
  boysenberries)

⅛ teaspoon salt
1¼ cups granulated sugar
1½ tablespoons fresh
  lemon juice

1. In a saucepan, combine gelatin and water. Let stand for 5 minutes and then heat gently until gelatin dissolves. Remove from heat.

2. Add puréed boysenberries, salt, sugar, and lemon juice to the dissolved gelatin. (To purée boysenberries, use an electric blender on medium speed.) Cool.

3. Churn-freeze.

Makes ½ gallon

Burgundy Wine Sherbet

2¾ cups cold water
1 cinnamon stick (1
  inch)
1½ cups granulated sugar
⅛ teaspoon salt
¼ cup applejack

2 cups red Burgundy
  wine
1 tablespoon fresh
  lemon juice
1 tablespoon finely
  grated orange rind

1. In a saucepan, mix together water, cinnamon stick, sugar, salt, and applejack. Boil for 5 minutes. Strain and cool.

2. Add wine, lemon juice, and grated orange rind to the cooled syrup. Chill in the refrigerator for 2 hours before freezing.

3. Churn-freeze.

Makes ½ gallon

Cantaloupe Sherbet

3 cups water
1½ cups granulated sugar
4 cups fresh cantaloupe
  pulp (about 2
  medium-size melons,
  2¼ pounds each)

2 tablespoons fresh
  lemon juice

1. In a saucepan, combine water and sugar. Boil for 5 minutes. Cool.
2. Remove cantaloupe from shell and purée in an electric blender on high speed.
3. Add cantaloupe pulp and lemon juice to sugar syrup.
4. Churn-freeze.

Makes ½ gallon

Carbonated Orange Sherbet

6 bottles carbonated
  orange drink
  (10-ounce size)

1 cup canned crushed
  pineapple, drained

1. Combine orange drink and drained crushed pineapple.
2. Churn-freeze.

Makes ½ gallon

Cassis Sherbet

1 cup granulated sugar
2½ cups water
1 cup red currant jelly

4 tablespoons fresh
  lemon juice
2 cups French cassis

1. In a saucepan, combine sugar and water. Boil for 5 minutes. Remove from heat.
2. Add jelly to hot sugar syrup. Cool.
3. Add lemon juice and cassis to the cooled mixture.
4. Churn-freeze.

Makes ½ gallon

Champagne Sherbet

2½ cups granulated sugar
 2 cups water
 3 cups sparkling
    champagne

Juice of 2 lemons
 4 egg whites, stiffly
    beaten

1. In a saucepan, combine sugar and water. Boil for 5 minutes. Cool.
2. Add champagne and juice of the lemons to the cooled sugar syrup.
3. Churn-freeze to mush.
4. Add stiffly beaten egg whites.
5. Churn-freeze until firm.

Makes ½ gallon

Cherry Sherbet

 4 cups water
1¾ cups granulated sugar
 2 cups fresh or canned
    cherry juice

⅛ teaspoon salt
 1 tablespoon fresh
    lemon juice

1. In a saucepan, combine water and sugar. Boil for 5 minutes. Cool.
2. Mix together sugar syrup, cherry juice, salt, and lemon juice. (Fresh cherry juice may be obtained by puréing fresh cherries in an electric blender, or by pressing

cherries through a sieve and then straining through cheesecloth.)
3. Churn-freeze.

Makes ½ gallon

Cherry Brandy Sherbet

1½ cups granulated sugar   2 tablespoons brandy
2½ cups water
3 cups fresh red
  cherries, pitted

1. In a saucepan, combine sugar and 1½ cups of the water. Boil for 5 minutes. Cool.
2. In another saucepan, combine remaining 1 cup water and the cherries. Cook just until cherries soften. Then press cherries through a sieve.
3. Mix together sugar syrup, cherry purée, and brandy.
4. Churn-freeze.

Makes ½ gallon

Cherry Kirsch Sherbet

1½ cups granulated sugar   ¾ cup light honey
1½ cups Sauterne   4 tablespoons kirsch
3 cups fresh black   ⅛ teaspoon salt
  cherries, pitted

1. In a saucepan, combine sugar and Sauterne. Boil for 3 minutes. Cool.
2. Purée cherries in an electric blender or press them through a sieve and then strain through a cheesecloth to obtain cherry juice.
3. Mix together sugar syrup, cherry juice, honey, kirsch, and salt.
4. Churn-freeze.

Makes ½ gallon

Chocolate Sherbet

2 cups granulated sugar   ¼ teaspoon ground
5 cups water   cinnamon
1 cup cocoa

1. In a saucepan, combine sugar and water. Boil for 5 minutes. Remove from heat.
2. Add cocoa and cinnamon to hot sugar syrup. Mix well. Cool.
3. Churn-freeze.

Makes ½ gallon

Cider Sherbet

5 cups cider   1½ cups fresh orange juice
2 tablespoons fresh   1 cup granulated sugar
   lemon juice

1. Mix together cider, lemon juice, orange juice, and sugar.
2. Churn-freeze.

Makes ½ gallon

Coffee Sherbet

4 cups water   1 egg white, stiffly
½ cup granulated sugar   beaten
4 tablespoons ground
   coffee

1. In a saucepan, combine water and sugar. Boil for 5 minutes. Remove from heat.

2. Add ground coffee to hot sugar syrup. Cover pan and let stand for 10 minutes. Strain and cool.

3. Add stiffly beaten egg white to cooled coffee mixture.

4. Churn-freeze.

Makes ½ gallon

Cola Sherbet

1 cup granulated sugar	5 bottles cola (12-ounce
¾ cup water	size)
½ cup fresh lemon juice	

1. In a saucepan, mix together sugar and water. Boil 5 minutes. Cool.
2. Combine cooled sugar syrup, lemon juice, and cola.
3. Churn-freeze.

Makes ½ gallon

Cranberry Sherbet I

1 tablespoon unflavored gelatin	4 cups fresh or canned cranberry juice
¼ cup cold water	3 tablespoons fresh lemon juice
1½ cups boiling water	
2 cups granulated sugar	

1. Dissolve gelatin in cold water. Let stand for 5 minutes.
2. Add boiling water, sugar, cranberry juice, and lemon juice to the gelatin. Strain and cool.
3. Churn-freeze.

Makes ½ gallon

Cranberry Sherbet II

2 cups granulated sugar	½ cup canned or fresh grapefruit juice
2 cups water	
3½ cups fresh cranberries	

1. Cook sugar, water, and cranberries for 15 minutes on low heat. Cool.
2. Add grapefruit juice to cranberry mixture and blend in electric blender for 2 minutes or purée in a food mill.
3. Still-freeze.

Makes ½ gallon

Cranberry Sherbet III

4 cups fresh cranberries
1 teaspoon ground
  cinnamon
2¾ cups water
1 tablespoon unflavored
  gelatin

⅓ cup cold water
2 tablespoons liquid
  Sucaryl (or 1 cup
  sugar)
2 teaspoons fresh lemon
  juice

1. Cook cranberries with cinnamon and 2¾ cups water until berries pop.
2. Purée berries in electric blender and return to saucepan.
3. Soften gelatin in ⅓ cup cold water.
4. Add Sucaryl, softened gelatin, and lemon juice to berries. Cook on low heat for 3 minutes. Cool.
5. Still-freeze until mushy.
6. Beat with rotary beater.
7. Still-freeze until firm.

Makes ½ gallon

Cranberry Pineapple Sherbet

3 cups fresh cranberries
1 cup water
2 cups canned
  unsweetened
  pineapple juice

20 marshmallows
1½ tablespoons fresh
  lemon juice
1 cup granulated sugar
⅛ teaspoon salt

1. In a saucepan, combine cranberries and water. Cook until the skins of the cranberries break. Remove from heat. Drain. Press cranberries through a sieve.
2. In another saucepan, combine pineapple juice and marshmallows. Heat until marshmallows melt.

3. Mix together sieved cranberries, pineapple-marsh-mallow mixture, lemon juice, sugar, and salt.
4. Churn-freeze.

Makes ½ gallon

Cucumber Sherbet

2 tablespoons
   unflavored gelatin
4 cups water
4 fresh apples, peeled
   and cored
4 large cucumbers,
   peeled

2 teaspoons granulated
   sugar
¼ teaspoon salt
½ teaspoon white pepper
2 tablespoons fresh
   lemon juice

1. Soften gelatin in ½ cup of the water. Let stand for 5 minutes, then heat gently until gelatin dissolves. Remove from heat.
2. Purée apples and cucumbers by using an electric blender or food mill.
3. Combine dissolved gelatin, apple and cucumber purée, remaining 3½ cups water, sugar, salt, pepper, and lemon juice.
4. Churn-freeze.

Makes ½ gallon

Currant Sherbet

1½ cups granulated sugar
3½ cups water
 ¼ cup fresh lemon juice

2 cups fresh currant
   juice

1. In a saucepan, combine sugar and water. Boil for 5 minutes. Cool.

2. Add lemon juice and currant juice to the cooled sugar syrup.

3. Churn-freeze.

Makes ½ gallon

Diabetic Orange Sherbet

6½ cups fresh orange juice   10   saccharin tablets
½ cup fresh lemon juice

1. Mix together orange juice, lemon juice, and saccharin tablets.

2. Churn-freeze.

Makes ½ gallon

Elderberry Rum Sherbet

3½ cups water   1½ tablespoons rum
1½ cups granulated sugar   1½ tablespoons orange
1½ pounds fresh ripe   flower water (see
     elderberries   page 46)
¼ cup fresh lemon juice

1. In a saucepan, combine 2 cups of the water and the sugar. Boil for 5 minutes. Cool.

2. In another saucepan, combine remaining 1½ cups water and elderberries. Cook, stirring, on low heat until elderberries turn into pulp. Strain. Add lemon juice. Cool.

3. Mix together sugar syrup, cooled, sieved elderberries, rum, and orange flower water.

4. Churn-freeze.

Makes ½ gallon

Forbidden Fruit Sherbet

16 large sugar lumps
 6 ripe oranges, washed
    and dried
 1 cup fresh orange juice,
    strained
1½ cups boiling water

½ cup Forbidden Fruit
   Liqueur
3 cups cold water
1⅓ cups granulated sugar
1 teaspoon grated lemon
   rind

1. Rub the sugar lumps on the washed and dried surfaces of the oranges.
2. Add orange juice, boiling water, and Forbidden Fruit Liqueur to the rubbed sugar lumps. Mix well. (Orange juice may be made from oranges used in step 1.)
3. Add cold water, granulated sugar, and lemon rind to the mixture. Chill in refrigerator for 1 hour and then strain.
4. Churn-freeze.

Makes ½ gallon

Fruit Cocktail Sherbet

1 cup canned fruit
   cocktail, drained
1 cup canned crushed
   pineapple, drained
1 cup granulated sugar
3 bananas, peeled and
   puréed

2 tablespoons fresh
   lemon juice
¼ cup fresh orange juice
2 cups ginger ale

1. Combine fruit cocktail, crushed pineapple, sugar, banana purée, lemon juice, orange juice, and ginger ale. Mix well.
2. Churn-freeze.

Makes ½ gallon

Fruit Kummel Sherbet

4 egg yolks, beaten
1 cup granulated sugar
⅛ teaspoon salt
6 large bananas, peeled
   and mashed
2 teaspoons fresh lemon
   juice

1½ cups fresh orange juice
2 cups canned crushed
   pineapple, undrained
4 egg whites, beaten
4 tablespoons kummel

1. Mix together beaten egg yolks, sugar, salt, mashed bananas, lemon juice, orange juice, and pineapple.
2. Add beaten egg whites and kummel.
3. Churn-freeze.

Makes ½ gallon

World's Speediest Sherbet: Fruit Sherbet

4 cans frozen
   concentrated fruit
   juice (6-ounce size)

4 cups crushed ice
3 egg whites

1. In electric blender, combine frozen fruit juice, crushed ice, and egg whites. Blend on high speed for 2 minutes.
2. Serve immediately.

Makes ½ gallon

Delicious and an exception to the rule that sherbets must be made ahead of time. Flavors are as varied as the wide selection of frozen concentrates.

Fruit Three Sherbet

3 cups water
3 cups granulated sugar
3 bananas, peeled and
  puréed
Juice of 3 lemons

Juice of 3 oranges
3 egg whites, stiffly
  beaten

1. In a saucepan, combine water and sugar. Boil for 5 minutes. Cool.
2. Mix sugar syrup with banana purée, juice of the lemons and oranges, and stiffly beaten egg whites.
3. Churn-freeze.

Makes ½ gallon

Ginger Sherbet

3 cups water
1½ cups granulated sugar
6 ounces preserved
  ginger in syrup

¾ cup fresh orange juice
½ cup fresh lemon juice
2 egg whites, beaten

1. In a saucepan, combine water and sugar. Boil for 5 minutes.
2. Using a mortar and pestle, grind preserved ginger with ginger syrup until smooth.
3. Add ginger, orange juice, and lemon juice to hot sugar syrup. Bring to a boil. Cool and strain.
4. Fold beaten egg whites into cooled mixture.
5. Churn-freeze.

Makes ½ gallon

Ginger Ale Sherbet

¾ cup granulated sugar
2 cups water
1 cup fresh orange juice

½ cup fresh lemon juice
3 bottles ginger ale
(10-ounce size)

1. In a saucepan, mix together sugar and water. Boil for 5 minutes. Cool.
2. Combine cooled sugar syrup, orange and lemon juices, and ginger ale.
3. Churn-freeze.

Makes ½ gallon

Ginger Ale Punch Sherbet

1 cup water
1 tablespoon unflavored
    gelatin
¾ cup granulated sugar
¼ cup fresh orange juice
6 tablespoons fresh
    lemon juice

¼ cup canned un-
    sweetened pineapple
    juice
4 cups ginger ale

1. In a saucepan, combine water and gelatin. Let stand for 5 minutes, then add sugar and heat, stirring, until gelatin dissolves. Cool.
2. Add orange, lemon, and pineapple juices and ginger ale to the cooled mixture.
3. Churn-freeze.

Makes ½ gallon

Gooseberry Jam Sherbet

2 cups gooseberry jam
¾ cup granulated sugar

4 cups water
¼ cup fresh lemon juice

1. Combine jam, sugar, water, and lemon juice. Mix well.
2. Churn-freeze.

Makes ½ gallon

Grape Sherbet

4 cups fresh grape juice
½ cup granulated sugar
¼ cup light corn syrup
3 egg whites

1. Mix together grape juice, sugar, and corn syrup.
2. Beat egg whites until stiff and fold whites into the grape mixture.
3. Churn-freeze.

Makes ½ gallon

Grape Juice Sherbet

2 cups water
1½ cups granulated sugar
¼ cup fresh lemon juice
3 cups fresh grape juice

1. In a saucepan, combine water and sugar. Boil for 5 minutes. Cool.
2. Add lemon juice and grape juice to the cooled sugar syrup.
3. Churn-freeze.

Makes ½ gallon

Grape Orange Sherbet

2 tablespoons un-
flavored gelatin
3 cups water
1½ cups granulated sugar
2 cups canned grape juice
1 cup fresh orange juice
2 tablespoons fresh lemon juice

1. Soften gelatin in ½ cup water.
2. In a saucepan, combine remaining water and sugar. Heat to a boil.
3. Add softened gelatin to hot sugar syrup. Cool to lukewarm.
4. Add grape juice, orange juice, and lemon juice to lukewarm mixture.
5. Churn-freeze.

Makes ½ gallon

Grapefruit Sherbet

1 tablespoon unflavored
  gelatin
¼ cup cold water
2 cups granulated sugar

1 cup hot water
5 cups fresh grapefruit
  juice
⅛ teaspoon salt

1. Soften gelatin in cold water.
2. In a saucepan, combine sugar and hot water. Boil for 2 minutes. Remove from heat.
3. Add softened gelatin to the hot mixture, then add grapefruit juice and salt. Cool.
4. Churn-freeze.

Makes ½ gallon

Prepared the night before, this makes a good starter on a hot summer day. It is especially pleasant served on a slice of cold melon.

Grape Marsala Sherbet

3 cups water
1½ cups granulated sugar
1½ pounds fresh grapes
½ cup Marsala wine

Juice of 2 lemons
1 tablespoon orange
  flower water (see
  page 46)

1. In a saucepan, combine water and sugar. Boil for 5 minutes. Cool.

2. Mash the grapes and then press through a sieve to remove seeds and skins.

3. Combine grape pulp, cooled sugar syrup, Marsala wine, juice of the lemons, and orange flower water.

4. Churn-freeze.

Makes ½ gallon

Seedless white grapes are good for this sherbet, but any kind of grape could be used.

Honeydew Melon Sherbet

2 honeydew melons, peeled and seeded	1½ cups granulated sugar
3 tablespoons fresh lemon juice	⅛ teaspoon salt
4 cups water	¾ cup dry or sweet sherry
	2 egg whites

1. Purée meat of the melon by forcing through a sieve or using an electric blender.

2. Combine melon purée with lemon juice.

3. In a saucepan, combine water, sugar, and salt. Boil for 5 minutes. Cool for 5 minutes.

4. Add sugar syrup and sherry to melon purée.

5. Beat egg whites until stiff and add to melon mixture. Mix well.

6. Churn-freeze or still-freeze, beating every 30 minutes.

Makes ½ gallon

Jam Sherbet

1½ pounds fruit jam	¼ cup confectioners' sugar
4 cups water	
3 tablespoons fresh lemon juice	

1. In a saucepan, combine jam, water, lemon juice, and sugar. Cook, stirring, until well combined. Cool.
2. Churn-freeze.

Makes ½ gallon

Kirsch Sherbet

1½ cups granulated sugar
4 cups water
3 tablespoons fresh
  lemon juice

½ cup kirsch liqueur
4 egg whites, beaten

1. In a saucepan, combine sugar and water. Boil for 5 minutes. Cool.
2. Add lemon juice, kirsch, and beaten egg whites to the sugar syrup.
3. Churn-freeze.

Makes ½ gallon

Kirsch Pineapple Sherbet

3 cups granulated sugar
1 cup water
¾ cup kirsch
3 cups shredded fresh
  pineapple

3 tablespoons fresh
  lemon juice
4 egg whites, stiffly
  beaten
2 tablespoons brandy

1. In a saucepan, combine sugar, water and kirsch. Boil for 5 minutes. Remove from heat.
2. Add pineapple and lemon juice to the hot mixture. Cool.
3. Stir stiffly beaten egg whites and brandy into the cooled mixture.
4. Still-freeze to mush.
5. Beat.
6. Still-freeze until firm.

Makes ½ gallon

Lemon Sherbet I

2 cups granulated sugar   1 cup fresh lemon juice
4 cups water

1. In a saucepan, combine sugar and water. Boil for 5 minutes. Cool.
2. Add lemon juice to cooled sugar syrup.
3. Churn-freeze.

Makes ½ gallon

Lemon Sherbet II

1 tablespoon unflavored   ⅛ teaspoon salt
   gelatin   ⅔ cup fresh lemon juice
4 cups plus 4 table-   4 egg whites, stiffly
   spoons water   beaten
1½ cups granulated sugar
2 teaspoons grated
   lemon rind

1. Soften gelatin in 4 tablespoons water.
2. In a saucepan, mix together 4 cups water, sugar, and grated lemon rind. Bring to boil and then allow mixture to simmer for 10 minutes.
3. Add softened gelatin and salt to hot sugar syrup. Mix well. Strain mixture and cool slightly.
4. Add lemon juice to cooled mixture.
5. Still-freeze to mush.
6. Beat mush with rotary beater, adding stiffly beaten egg whites.
7. Still-freeze until firm.

Makes ½ gallon

Lime Sherbet

1 tablespoon unflavored gelatin	¼ teaspoon green food coloring
4½ cups plus 4 table-spoons cold water	4 egg whites, stiffly beaten
2 cups granulated sugar	⅛ teaspoon salt
Juice of 12 limes	

1. Soften gelatin in 4 tablespoons cold water.
2. In a saucepan, combine sugar and 4½ cups water. Bring to a boil, then allow mixture to simmer for 10 minutes.
3. Add softened gelatin to hot sugar syrup. Cool slightly.
4. Squeeze limes, adding lime juice and green food coloring to the cooled mixture. Mix well.
5. Still-freeze to mush.
6. Beat mush with rotary beater, folding in stiffly beaten egg whites and the salt.
7. Still-freeze until firm.

Makes ½ gallon

Mango Sherbet

1 cup granulated sugar	4 tablespoons fresh lemon juice
3 cups water	3 egg whites, stiffly beaten
3 cups fresh mango purée (about 3 medium-size mangoes, or 1¾ pounds)	

1. In a saucepan, combine sugar and water. Boil for 5 minutes. Cool.
2. Combine mango purée, lemon juice, and sugar syrup. (To purée mangoes, use electric blender on medium speed, or mash with wooden potato masher.)

3. Add stiffly beaten egg whites.
4. Churn-freeze.

Makes ½ gallon

Maraschino Sherbet

2 cups granulated sugar
3 cups water
½ cup fresh lemon juice
½ cup fresh orange juice

¾ cup maraschino
   liqueur
3 tablespoons kirsch
   (optional)

1. In a saucepan, combine sugar and water. Boil for 5 minutes. Cool.
2. Add lemon juice, orange juice, maraschino liqueur, and kirsch to the cooled sugar syrup.
3. Churn-freeze.

Makes ½ gallon

√ Melon Sherbet

6 cups melon purée
   (about 1 large water-
   melon or 3 medium-
   sized cantaloupes)
2 tablespoons
   unflavored gelatin

1½ cups granulated sugar
 2 tablespoons fresh
    lemon juice
 ¼ teaspoon salt

1. Purée melon by using an electric blender on medium-speed or food mill.
2. Soften gelatin in ¼ cup of the melon purée. Let stand for 5 minutes, then heat gently until dissolved.
3. Combine melon purée, dissolved gelatin, sugar, lemon juice, and salt.
4. Churn-freeze.

Makes ½ gallon

A watermelon shell filled with this delicious sherbet and decorated with chocolate chips for seeds is a wonderful summertime barbecue dessert. This recipe can be used for cantaloupe, except that it is necessary to add ¼ cup water for softening the gelatin.

Mexican Tequila Sherbet

3 cups water
2 cups granulated sugar
⅓ cup fresh lime juice
⅓ cup tequila
¼ teaspoon green food
    coloring

3 egg whites, stiffly
    beaten
¼ teaspoon salt

1. In a saucepan, combine water and sugar. Boil for 5 minutes. Remove from heat.
2. Add lime juice, tequila, and green food coloring to the warm mixture. Cool.
3. Add stiffly beaten egg whites and salt to the cooled mixture.
4. Churn-freeze.

Makes ½ gallon

Mint Sherbet

1 cup fresh mint leaves
2 cups granulated sugar
2 cups water
Juice of 4 lemons
Juice of 1 orange

Juice of 1 lime
¼ teaspoon green food
    coloring
2 egg whites, stiffly
    beaten

1. Chop mint into fine pieces.
2. In a saucepan, combine sugar and 1 cup of the water and bring to a boil.
3. Add half of the chopped mint to the boiling sugar syrup and continue to boil for 3 minutes. Strain and cool.
4. Squeeze lemons, orange, and lime.
5. Add the citrus juices, green food coloring, remaining chopped mint, remaining 1 cup water, and the stiffly beaten egg whites to the cooled mixture.
6. Churn-freeze.

Makes ½ gallon

Mint Julep Sherbet

¾ cup chopped mint
   leaves
2 cups boiling water
1½ cups granulated sugar
2 tablespoons
   unflavored gelatin
¼ cup cold water

1½ cups canned grape
   juice (or cherry juice)
¾ cup fresh strawberry
   juice
¼ cup fresh lemon juice
¾ cup fresh orange juice
2 egg whites

1. Pour boiling water over chopped mint and let stand for 5 minutes. Strain.

2. In a saucepan, combine sugar and strained mint water and boil for 5 minutes.

3. Soften gelatin in the ¼ cup cold water.

4. Add hot sugar-mint water to the softened gelatin. Cool slightly.

5. Add grape, strawberry, lemon, and orange juices to cooled mixture. Mix well.

6. Still-freeze to mush.

7. Beat egg whites until stiff and then add to the mushy sherbet, beating well.

8. Still-freeze until firm.

Makes ½ gallon

Mixed Fruit Sherbet

4 packages frozen mixed
   fruits (12-ounce size),
   thawed, with juice
1 cup granulated sugar
2 teaspoons unflavored
   gelatin

¼ cup cold water
4 tablespoons fresh
   lemon juice
1 teaspoon grated lemon
   peel

1. Drain the thawed mixed fruits, reserving 1¼ cups of the juice.

2. In an electric blender, blend mixed fruits until smooth.

3. In a saucepan, mix together fruit purée, sugar, and 1¼ cups reserved juice. Cook, stirring, until mixture comes to a boil.

4. Soften gelatin in cold water.

5. Add gelatin to the hot fruit mixture. Mix well. Cool.

6. Add lemon juice and grated lemon peel to the cooled mixture. Mix well.

7. Churn-freeze or still-freeze to mush. Beat and still-freeze until firm.

Makes ½ gallon

Mulberry Sherbet

3 cups water
1½ cups granulated sugar
1 pound fresh ripe red
   mulberries, washed
½ pound fresh ripe red
   raspberries, washed

3 tablespoons fresh
   lemon juice
2 tablespoons brandy

1. In a saucepan, combine water and sugar. Boil for 5 minutes. Cool.

2. Combine washed mulberries and raspberries and purée by pressing through a sieve or using an electric blender. Strain.

3. Mix together cooled sugar syrup, mulberry-raspberry purée, lemon juice, and brandy.

4. Churn-freeze.

Makes ½ gallon

Muscatel Apricot Sherbet

3½ cups canned apricots,   1½ cups boiling water
     undrained   Juice of 1 lemon
 ½ cup granulated sugar   ⅛ teaspoon salt
 ½ cup dark brown sugar,   ¾ cup muscatel wine
     firmly packed

1. Purée apricots in electric blender, retaining juice.
2. Add white and brown sugars to boiling water and stir until sugar dissolves. Cool.
3. Combine, mixing well, apricots, cooled sugar syrup, juice of the lemon, salt, and muscatel wine.
4. Churn-freeze.

Makes ½ gallon

Nectarine Sherbet

1½ cups granulated sugar   1 tablespoon kirsch
 4 cups water   (optional)
1½ pounds fresh ripe   ⅛ teaspoon red food
     nectarines, peeled and   coloring
     pitted
 2 tablespoons fresh
     lemon juice

1. In a saucepan, combine sugar and water. Boil for 5 minutes.
2. Purée the peeled and pitted nectarines.
3. Add the nectarine purée to the hot sugar syrup. Simmer for 15 minutes. Cool.
4. Add the lemon juice, kirsch, and red food coloring to the cooled mixture.
5. Churn-freeze.

Makes ½ gallon

Orange Sherbet I

2¼ cups water
1½ cups granulated sugar
½ teaspoon finely grated orange rind
3 cups fresh orange juice
2 tablespoons fresh lemon juice

⅛ teaspoon cream of tartar
1 egg white, stiffly beaten
½ cup Cointreau

1. In a saucepan, combine 2 cups water and 1 cup sugar. Boil for 5 minutes.
2. Add orange rind, orange juice, and lemon juice to sugar syrup. Mix well. Cool and then strain.
3. Still-freeze to mush.
4. Prepare a second sugar syrup by combining remaining sugar and water and the cream of tartar in a saucepan. Boil for 5 minutes. Beat sugar syrup into stiffly beaten egg white. Beat mixture until cool.
5. Beat mush with a rotary beater, gradually adding stiffly beaten egg white mixture and Cointreau while beating.
6. Still-freeze until firm.

Makes ½ gallon

Orange Sherbet II

1½ cups granulated sugar
½ cup light corn syrup
3 cups water

¼ teaspoon salt
½ cup fresh lemon juice
2 cups fresh orange juice

1. In a saucepan, mix together sugar, corn syrup, water, and salt. Cook, stirring, on low heat for 5 minutes. Cool.
2. Add lemon juice and orange juice to the cooled mixture.
3. Churn-freeze.

Makes ½ gallon

Orange Chocolate Sherbet

1 tablespoon unflavored
gelatin
3½ cups water
2 cups granulated sugar
6 ounces semisweet
chocolate

1 cup fresh orange juice
1 teaspoon vanilla
extract

1. Soften gelatin in ½ cup of the water.
2. In a saucepan, combine remaining 3 cups water and the sugar. Boil for 5 minutes. Remove from heat.
3. Add softened gelatin to hot sugar syrup.
4. In top of double boiler, melt chocolate.
5. Beating vigorously, mix together sugar syrup and melted chocolate.
6. Add orange juice and vanilla to the mixture.
7. Churn-freeze.

Makes ½ gallon

Orgeat Sherbet

4 cups water
2 cups granulated sugar
1 pound blanched
almonds, ground
2 tablespoons orange
flower water (see
page 46)

2 teaspoons crème de
noyau liqueur

1. In a saucepan, combine 2 cups of the water and the sugar. Boil for 5 minutes. Cool.
2. In another saucepan, combine ground almonds and remaining 2 cups water. Let simmer for ½ hour, stirring occasionally. Cool.

3. Mix together sugar syrup, cooled almonds, orange flower water, and crème de noyau liqueur.

4. Churn-freeze.

Makes ½ gallon

Papaya Sherbet

6 *fresh ripe papayas*   2½ *cups granulated sugar*
¼ *cup fresh lemon juice*

1. Peel and remove seeds from the papayas.
2. In an electric blender, combine papaya pulp and lemon juice. Blend until smooth.
3. Add sugar to the papaya purée. Mix well.
4. Churn-freeze.

Makes ½ gallon

Peach Sherbet

4½ *cups fresh peach pulp*   ⅛ *teaspoon salt*
    purée (about 4½   2½ *teaspoons almond*
    pounds peaches)   *extract*
2½ *teaspoons fresh lemon*   2½ *teaspoons vanilla*
    juice   *extract*
1½ *cups confectioners'*   6 *egg whites, beaten*
    sugar

1. Mix together peach purée, lemon juice, sugar, salt, almond extract, and vanilla extract. (To purée peaches, use an electric blender on medium speed.)
2. Stir beaten egg whites into mixture.
3. Churn-freeze.

Makes ½ gallon

Peach Orange Sherbet

3½ cups fresh peach pulp   ¾ cup granulated sugar
    purée (about 3½   2 tablespoons fresh
    pounds peaches)   lemon juice
2¼ cups fresh orange juice

1. Mix together peach purée, orange juice, sugar, and lemon juice. (To purée peaches, use an electric blender on medium speed.)
2. Churn-freeze.

Makes ½ gallon

Pear Sherbet

3½ cups water   1 cinnamon stick (2
 1 cup granulated sugar   inches)
 6 fresh ripe pears,   3 tablespoons fresh
    peeled, cored, and   lemon juice
    sliced

1. In a saucepan, combine water and sugar. Boil for 5 minutes.
2. Add peeled, cored, sliced pears and cinnamon to the hot sugar syrup. Cook, stirring occasionally, on low heat until pears are tender. Strain mixture through a sieve. Cool.
3. Add lemon juice to the cooled mixture.
4. Churn-freeze.

Makes ½ gallon

Peppermint Grapefruit Sherbet

2 tablespoons unflavored gelatin	2 cups granulated sugar
4 cups fresh grapefruit juice	½ teaspoon oil of peppermint
2 cups water	¼ teaspoon green food coloring

1. Soften gelatin in 3 tablespoons of the grapefruit juice.
2. In a saucepan, combine water and sugar. Boil for 5 minutes. Remove from heat.
3. Add softened gelatin to the hot sugar syrup. Cool slightly.
4. Add remaining grapefruit juice, the oil of peppermint, and green food coloring to the gelatin-sugar mixture.
5. Churn-freeze.

Makes ½ gallon

Pineapple Sherbet I

2 cups grated fresh pineapple	1 teaspoon finely grated lemon rind
2 cups canned unsweetened pineapple juice	2 cups water
	2 cups granulated sugar

1. In a saucepan, mix together all ingredients. Boil for 5 minutes. Strain. Cool.
2. Churn-freeze.

Makes ½ gallon

Pineapple Sherbet II

1½ cups water
1½ cups granulated sugar
1 tablespoon unflavored gelatin
¼ cup cold water
¼ cup plus 2 tablespoons fresh lemon juice

3⅓ cups canned unsweetened pineapple juice
3 egg whites

1. Boil the 1½ cups water and the sugar together for 10 minutes.
2. Soften gelatin in the ¼ cup water and add gelatin mixture to hot sugar syrup. Cool slightly.
3. Add lemon juice and pineapple juice to gelatin mixture. Mix well.
4. Still-freeze to mush.
5. Beat egg whites until stiff and then add egg whites to mushy sherbet. Mix well.
6. Still-freeze until firm.

Makes ½ gallon

Pineapple Banana Sherbet

1 cup granulated sugar
3 cups canned or fresh crushed pineapple, drained
1½ cups banana pulp (about 6 bananas)

⅔ cup fresh orange juice
2 tablespoons fresh lemon juice
2 egg whites
⅛ teaspoon salt

1. Combine sugar and crushed pineapple and refrigerate for 1 hour.
2. Purée bananas in a blender or by pressing through a sieve.

3. Add orange juice and lemon juice to bananas and then add to pineapple mixture. Mix well.

4. Still-freeze to mush.

5. Beat the egg whites with salt until stiff and then add to the mushy sherbet, beating well.

6. Still-freeze until firm.

Makes ½ gallon

Pineapple Mint Sherbet

2 tablespoons unflavored gelatin
½ cup water
3½ cups canned unsweetened pineapple juice
1 cup granulated sugar

2 tablespoons fresh mint, finely chopped
2 cups canned crushed pineapple, drained
3 tablespoons fresh lemon juice

1. Soften gelatin in water.

2. In a saucepan, combine pineapple juice and sugar. Heat until sugar melts.

3. Add gelatin and mint to hot pineapple juice. Cool.

4. Add crushed pineapple and lemon juice to cooled mixture.

5. Churn-freeze.

Makes ½ gallon

Pineapple, Mint, and Ginger Ale Sherbet

1 cup granulated sugar
1 cup water
⅛ teaspoon green food coloring
¼ teaspoon mint flavoring

⅓ cup fresh lemon juice
1¾ cups canned crushed pineapple, drained
2½ cups ginger ale

1. In a saucepan, combine sugar and water. Boil for 5 minutes.
2. Add food coloring, mint flavoring, lemon juice, crushed pineapple, and ginger ale to the sugar syrup.
3. Churn-freeze.

Makes ½ gallon

Pistachio Sherbet

4 cups water
2 cups granulated sugar
1 cup blanched
   pistachio nuts, ground
2 tablespoons orange
   flower water (see
   page 46)

2 tablespoons
   maraschino liqueur
2 tablespoons kirsch
½ teaspoon green food
   coloring

1. In a saucepan, mix together water and sugar. Boil 5 minutes. Cool.
2. Mix together cooled sugar syrup, ground pistachio nuts, orange flower water, maraschino liqueur, kirsch, and green food coloring.
3. Churn-freeze.

Makes ½ gallon

Plum Sherbet

3¾ cups water
 2 cups granulated sugar
 2 cups cooked fresh
   plum purée (about 8
   medium-size plums, or
   2 pounds)

1 tablespoon fresh
   lemon juice

1. In a saucepan, combine water and sugar. Boil for 5 minutes. Cool.

2. Mix together cooled sugar syrup, cooked plum purée, and lemon juice. To purée plums: peel, pit, and blend in an electric blender on medium speed.

3. Churn-freeze.

Makes ½ gallon

Pomegranate Sherbet

2 cups granulated sugar
3 cups water
8 large fresh ripe
   pomegranates
2 tablespoons fresh
   lemon juice

¾ cup fresh orange juice
   and pulp
2 teaspoons curaçao
   (optional)

1. In a saucepan, combine sugar and water. Boil for 5 minutes.

2. Split the pomegranates, remove the seeds and pulp. Then press seeds and pulp through a potato masher.

3. Add the lemon juice, orange juice and pulp, and pressed pomegranates to the sugar syrup in the saucepan. Simmer, stirring occasionally, for 15 minutes. Cool.

4. Add the curaçao to the cooled mixture.

5. Churn-freeze.

Makes ½ gallon

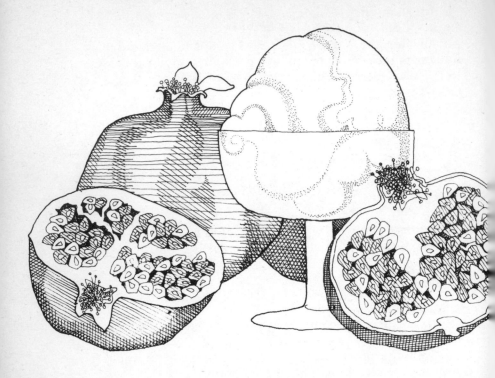

Popsicles

4 cups fresh fruit purée   2 cups fresh orange juice
¾ cup granulated sugar

1. Combine fruit purée, sugar, and orange juice. Mix well. (Any kind of fruit may be used for the purée.)
2. Still-freeze in ice cube tray until mushy.
3. Stand a wooden picnic spoon in each cube.
4. Still-freeze until firm.

Makes ½ gallon

Special forms for freezing Popsicles can be purchased in some housewares departments.

Port Lime Sherbet

3 *cups water*
1¼ *cups granulated sugar*
⅛ *teaspoon salt*

2 *cups port wine*
¼ *cup fresh lime juice*

1. In a saucepan, combine water, sugar, and salt. Boil for 5 minutes. Remove from heat.
2. Add port and lime juice to the hot sugar syrup. Cool.
3. Churn-freeze.

Makes ½ gallon

Port Wine Sherbet

3 *cups water*
1½ *cups granulated sugar*
⅛ *teaspoon salt*
2 *cups port wine*

¼ *cup fresh lemon juice*
4 *egg whites, stiffly beaten*

1. In a saucepan, combine water, sugar, and salt. Boil for 5 minutes.
2. Add port and lemon juice to hot sugar syrup. Mix well. Cool.
3. Still-freeze to mush.
4. Beat, adding stiffly beaten egg whites while beating.
5. Still-freeze until firm.

Makes ½ gallon

Punch Sherbet

3 *cups water*
2 *cups granulated sugar*
1 *cup fresh orange juice*
¼ *cup strong tea liquid*

⅓ *cup fresh lemon juice*
¼ *cup brandy*
¼ *cup curaçao*

1. In a saucepan, combine water and sugar. Boil for 5 minutes. Cool.
2. Add orange juice, tea, and lemon juice to the cooled sugar syrup.
3. Churn-freeze to mush.
4. Add brandy and curaçao to contents in freezer can.
5. Churn-freeze until firm.

Makes ½ gallon

Raspberry Sherbet

3 cups water
1½ cups granulated sugar
3 cups raspberry purée (about 1 full quart raspberries)

2 teaspoons fresh lemon juice
2 tablespoons crème de framboise (raspberry liqueur)

1. In a saucepan, combine water and sugar. Boil for 5 minutes. Cool.
2. Mix together raspberry purée, lemon juice, crème de framboise, and cooled sugar syrup. (To purée raspberries, use an electric blender on medium speed.)
3. Churn-freeze.

Makes ½ gallon

Raspberry Currant Sherbet

1 tablespoon unflavored gelatin
¼ cup cold water
2 cups juice drained from canned raspberries

2 cups currant jelly
3½ cups water

1. Soften gelatin in the ¼ cup cold water for 5 minutes.
2. In a saucepan, combine raspberry juice, currant jelly, and the 3½ cups water. Cook, stirring, on low heat until jelly dissolves.
3. Add softened gelatin to hot mixture. Mix well. Cool.
4. Churn-freeze.

Makes ½ gallon

Red Cherry Sherbet

6 cups fresh red cherries, pitted	1 tablespoon unflavored gelatin
1¾ cups granulated sugar	⅔ cup fresh orange juice

1. Combine pitted fresh cherries with the sugar. Let stand for 1 hour.
2. Soften gelatin in the orange juice.
3. In a saucepan, combine gelatin-orange mixture with juice drained from cherries. Heat until gelatin dissolves.
4. Mix together cherries and gelatin mixture.
5. Churn-freeze.

Makes ½ gallon

Rhubarb Sherbet

2¾ cups granulated sugar	2 tablespoons fresh lemon juice
2½ cups water	4 egg whites, beaten
2½ cups cooked rhubarb purée (about 17 medium-size stalks, or 2½ pounds)	

1. In a saucepan, combine sugar and water. Boil for 5 minutes. Cool.
2. Add rhubarb purée and lemon juice to the cooled sugar syrup.

3. Fold beaten egg whites into the mixture.
4. Churn-freeze.

Makes ½ gallon

Before cooking rhubarb, remove the leaves and ends of the stems. (If the rhubarb is young and tender, it does not need to be peeled.) Cut stalks into short pieces and place in saucepan with water to cover. Cook on medium heat until tender. Drain. To purée the cooked rhubarb, force through a food mill.

Rhubarb Vodka Sherbet

2 tablespoons unflavored gelatin
¼ cup cold water
4 cups cooked rhubarb (about 28 medium-size stalks, or 4 pounds)

2½ cups granulated sugar
8 tablespoons vodka
4 egg whites, stiffly beaten

1. Soften gelatin in water.
2. In a saucepan, combine cooked rhubarb and sugar. Cook on medium heat until sugar melts. Remove from heat.
3. Add softened gelatin and vodka to hot rhubarb mixture. Chill in refrigerator until mixture thickens.
4. Add stiffly beaten egg whites to cooled rhubarb mixture.
5. Churn-freeze.

Makes ½ gallon

Roman Punch Sherbet

1¼ cups granulated sugar
Juice of 3 lemons
Juice of 3 oranges
2½ cups champagne

½ cup strong tea liquid
3 egg whites, stiffly
  beaten
1 cup rum

1. In a saucepan, combine sugar and juice of the lemons and oranges. Boil for 5 minutes. Cool.
2. Add champagne and tea to the cooled sugar syrup. Mix well.
3. Still-freeze to mush.
4. Beat, adding stiffly beaten egg whites and rum while beating.
5. Still-freeze until firm.

Makes ½ gallon

Root Beer Ice

½ cup granulated sugar
¼ cup fresh lemon juice

6 bottles root beer
  (10-ounce size)

1. Mix together sugar, lemon juice, and root beer.
2. Churn-freeze.

Makes ½ gallon

Sherry Sherbet

1½ tablespoons
unflavored gelatin
3¼ cups water
1½ cups granulated sugar
9 tablespoons fresh
lemon juice
¾ cup fresh orange juice

1½ cups dry or sweet
sherry
⅛ teaspoon red food
coloring
3 egg whites, stiffly
beaten

1. Soften gelatin in ¼ cup of the water.
2. In a saucepan, combine remaining 3 cups water and
the sugar. Boil for 5 minutes. Remove from heat.
3. Add softened gelatin to hot sugar syrup. Cool.

4. Add lemon juice, orange juice, sherry, red food coloring, and stiffly beaten egg whites to the cooled mixture.

5. Churn-freeze.

Makes ½ gallon

Although either dry or sweet sherry may be used, in this recipe it is preferable to use dry.

Sherry Melon Sherbet

2 cups water
1 cup granulated sugar
2½ cups honeydew melon purée (about 1 melon, or 3½ pounds)
2 tablespoons fresh lemon juice
⅛ teaspoon salt
¾ cup sherry

1. In a saucepan, combine water and sugar. Boil for 5 minutes. Cool.

2. Mix together cooled sugar syrup, melon purée, lemon juice, salt, and sherry. (To purée melon, use an electric blender on high speed.)

3. Churn-freeze.

Makes ½ gallon

Strawberry Sherbet

4½ cups fresh strawberries
1½ cups granulated sugar
1 teaspoon fresh lemon juice
⅛ teaspoon salt
1 cup water

1. Clean berries and slice in half.

2. Combine berries and sugar. Let stand for 2½ hours.

3. Purée berries in an electric blender on medium speed.

4. Add lemon juice, salt, and water to the berry purée.
5. Churn-freeze.

Makes ½ gallon

Strawberry Applesauce Sherbet

2 tablespoons unflavored gelatin	3½ cups fresh strawberry purée (about 1 full quart strawberries)
2 cups water	
2 cups granulated sugar	½ cup applesauce

1. Soften gelatin in ¼ cup water.
2. In a saucepan, combine the remaining water and the sugar. Boil for 5 minutes. Remove from heat.
3. Add the softened gelatin to the hot sugar syrup. Cool.
4. Add the strawberry purée and applesauce to the cooled sugar-gelatin syrup. (To purée strawberries, blend in an electric blender on medium speed.)
5. Churn-freeze.

Makes ½ gallon

Strawberry Apricot Brandy Sherbet

1½ cups granulated sugar	2 tablespoons fresh lemon juice
3½ cups cold water	
½ cup apricot brandy	½ teaspoon grated orange rind
⅛ teaspoon salt	
2 cups fresh strawberry juice (about 1½ pints strawberries)	

1. In a saucepan, combine sugar, water, and apricot brandy. Boil for 5 minutes. Cool.

2. Add salt, strawberry juice, lemon juice, and grated orange rind to the cooled sugar syrup.

3. Churn-freeze.

Makes ½ gallon

To obtain strawberry juice, purée fresh strawberries in an electric blender on medium speed, then strain through a fine sieve.

Strawberry Orange Sherbet

2½ cups water
1¾ cups granulated sugar
 ½ teaspoon unflavored
     gelatin
2½ cups fresh strawberry
     purée (about 1½ pints
     strawberries)

1½ tablespoons fresh
     lemon juice
 ¾ cup fresh orange juice
2   egg whites, stiffly
     beaten

1. In a saucepan, combine 2 cups of the water and the sugar. Boil for 10 minutes.

2. Soften gelatin in remaining water and add dissolved gelatin to hot sugar syrup. Cool.

3. Add puréed strawberries and lemon and orange juices to the cooled sugar syrup. (To purée strawberries, blend in an electric blender on medium speed.)

4. Churn-freeze to mush.

5. Open freezer and fold stiffly beaten egg whites into the mixture.

6. Churn-freeze until firm.

Makes ½ gallon

Strawberry Pineapple Sherbet

3 cups fresh
   strawberries, washed
   and hulled
1 cup granulated sugar
1½ cups water

2 cups canned crushed
   pineapple, drained
1 teaspoon fresh lemon
   juice

1. In an electric blender, combine the washed and hulled strawberries and sugar. Blend until well combined.
2. Add water, crushed pineapple, and the lemon juice to the strawberry purée.
3. Churn-freeze.

Makes ½ gallon

Tangerine Sherbet

2½ cups granulated sugar
2 cups water
2½ cups fresh tangerine
   juice
2 drops red food
   coloring

2 drops yellow food
   coloring
3 egg whites, stiffly
   beaten

1. In a saucepan, combine sugar and water. Boil for 5 minutes. Cool.
2. Add tangerine juice and food coloring to the sugar syrup. Mix well.
3. Still-freeze to mush.
4. Beat mush, adding stiffly beaten egg whites.
5. Still-freeze until firm.

Makes ½ gallon

Tea Sherbet

1½ cups water
1¼ cups granulated sugar

4½ cups strong tea liquid,
    cool

1. In a saucepan, combine water and sugar. Boil for 5 minutes. Cool.
2. Combine tea and cooled sugar syrup. Mix well.
3. Still-freeze or churn-freeze.

Makes ½ gallon

Tomato Sherbet

1 quart can tomatoes, drained, or 12 fresh tomatoes
1 slice onion
¼ teaspoon ground mace
1 teaspoon celery seed
2 cups water
1 teaspoon salt

1 teaspoon paprika
1 tablespoon unflavored gelatin
1 tablespoon fresh lemon juice
⅛ teaspoon cayenne pepper

1. In a saucepan, combine all ingredients. Bring to a boil and boil for 5 minutes, stirring occasionally. Strain and cool.
2. Churn-freeze.

Makes ½ gallon

Tomato Clove Sherbet

5½ cups canned tomatoes, undrained
12 cloves
12 peppercorns
 4 tablespoons granulated sugar

2 teaspoons salt
8 tablespoons finely minced onion

1. In a saucepan, combine tomatoes, cloves, pepper-corns, sugar, salt, and onion. Cook, stirring occasionally, on medium heat for 10 minutes. Press mixture through a sieve. Cool.
2. Churn-freeze.

Makes ½ gallon

Tomato Juice Sherbet

2 tablespoons
   unflavored gelatin
¼ cup water
7 cups fresh or canned
   tomato juice

3 tablespoons fresh
   lemon juice
¾ teaspoon salt
¼ teaspoon white pepper
3 egg whites

1. Soften gelatin in water.
2. In a saucepan, heat tomato juice to a boil. Remove from heat.
3. Add softened gelatin, lemon juice, salt, and pepper to the hot juice. Cool.
4. Stiffly beat egg whites and stir into tomato mixture.
5. Churn-freeze.

Makes ½ gallon

Tutti-Frutti Sherbet

¼ cup maraschino cherry
   juice
½ cup canned or fresh
   grapefruit juice
1½ cups fresh orange juice
2 cups canned crushed
   pineapple, drained
12 small marshmallows

12 maraschino cherries,
   sliced
1 cup canned shredded
   coconut
5 egg whites
¾ cup confectioners'
   sugar

1. Mix together cherry juice, grapefruit juice, orange juice, pineapple, marshmallows, cherries, and shredded coconut. Let stand at room temperature for 45 minutes.
2. Beat egg whites until stiff.
3. Add beaten egg whites and sugar to fruit mixture.
4. Churn-freeze.

Makes ½ gallon

Vanilla Sherbet

6½ cups water
 1 cup granulated sugar
 2 pieces vanilla bean
     (4-inch size), split

1½ tablespoons fresh
     lemon juice

1. In a saucepan, mix together water, sugar, and split vanilla beans. Boil for 10 minutes. Cool and strain.
2. Add lemon juice.
3. Churn-freeze.

Makes ½ gallon

White Wine Sherbet

2 tablespoons
    unflavored gelatin
2 cups water
1½ cups granulated sugar

4 cups dry white wine
¼ cup fresh lime juice
2 tablespoons crème de
    menthe

1. Soften gelatin in ¼ cup of the water.
2. In a saucepan, combine remaining 1¾ cups water and the sugar. Bring to a boil and then allow mixture to simmer for 10 minutes.
3. Add softened gelatin to the hot sugar syrup. Cool.
4. Add white wine, lime juice, and crème de menthe to the cooled mixture.
5. Churn-freeze.

Makes ½ gallon

Zabaglione Sherbet

4 tablespoons
   unflavored gelatin
1½ cups water

24 egg yolks
2 cups granulated sugar
1 cup Marsala wine

1. Soften gelatin in the water.
2. In top of a double boiler, combine egg yolks and sugar. Beat with rotary beater until well blended.
3. Add Marsala to the egg yolk–sugar mixture. Cook, while beating continuously, until mixture begins to foam and thicken, and then remove from heat immediately.
4. Add softened gelatin to the hot mixture. Beat vigorously.
5. Still-freeze.

Makes ½ gallon

Index